TRUSTING NUDGES

Many "nudges" aim to make life simpler, safer, or easier for people to navigate, but what do members of the public really think about these policies? Drawing on surveys from numerous nations around the world, Sunstein and Reisch explore whether citizens approve of nudge policies. Their most important finding is simple and striking. In diverse countries, both democratic and nondemocratic, strong majorities approve of nudges designed to promote health, safety, and environmental protection—and their approval cuts across political divisions.

In recent years, many governments have implemented behaviorally informed policies, focusing on nudges—understood as interventions that preserve freedom of choice, but that also steer people in certain directions. In some circles, nudges have become controversial, with questions raised about whether they amount to forms of manipulation. This fascinating book carefully considers these criticisms and answers important questions. What do citizens actually think about behaviorally informed policies? Do citizens have identifiable principles in mind when they approve or disapprove of the policies? Do citizens of different nations agree with each other?

From the answers to these questions, the authors identify six principles of legitimacy—a "bill of rights" for nudging that build on strong public support for nudging policies around the world, while also recognizing what citizens disapprove of. Their bill of rights is designed to capture citizens' central concerns, reflecting widespread commitments to freedom and welfare that transcend national boundaries.

Cass R. Sunstein is the Robert Walmsley University Professor at Harvard, USA. From 2009 to 2012, he was Administrator of the White House Office of Information and Regulatory Affairs. He is the founder and director of the Program on Behavioral Economics and Public Policy at Harvard Law School.

Lucia A. Reisch is a behavioral economist and Professor at Copenhagen Business School, Denmark. She also holds a permanent Guest Professorship at the Zeppelin University of Friedrichshafen, Germany, and an appointment as honorary Leibniz Chair, awarded by the German Leibniz Association and the Leibniz Institute of Prevention Research and Epidemiology.

ROUTLEDGE ADVANCES IN BEHAVIOURAL ECONOMICS AND FINANCE

Edited by Roger Frantz

Traditionally, economists have based their analysis of financial markets and corporate finance on the assumption that agents are fully rational, emotionless, self-interested maximizers of expected utility. However, behavioural economists are increasingly recognizing that financial decision makers may be subject to psychological biases, and the effects of emotions. Examples of this include the effects on investors' and managers' decision-making of such biases as excessive optimism, overconfidence, confirmation bias, and illusion of control. At a practical level, the current state of the financial markets suggests that trust between investors and managers is of paramount importance.

Routledge Advances in Behavioural Economics and Finance presents innovative and cutting-edge research in this fast-paced and rapidly growing area, and will be of great interest to academics, practitioners, and policy-makers alike.

All proposals for new books in the series can be sent to the series editor, Roger Frantz, at rabeandf@gmail.com.

1. **Behavioural Economics and Business Ethics**
   Interrelations and Applications
   Alexander Rajko

2. **Bounded Rationality and Behavioural Economics**
   Graham Mallard

3. **Behavioural Approaches to Corporate Governance**
   Cameron Elliott Gordon

4. **Trusting Nudges**
   Toward a Bill of Rights for Nudging
   Cass R. Sunstein and Lucia A. Reisch

For more information about this series, please visit: www.routledge.com/ Routledge-Advances-in-Behavioural-Economics-and-Finance/book-series/ RABEF

TRUSTING NUDGES

Toward a Bill of Rights for Nudging

Cass R. Sunstein and Lucia A. Reisch

Routledge
Taylor & Francis Group

LONDON AND NEW YORK

First published 2019
by Routledge

2 Park Square, Milton Park, Abingdon, Oxfordshire OX14 4RN
52 Vanderbilt Avenue, New York, NY 10017

Routledge is an imprint of the Taylor & Francis Group, an informa business

First issued in hardback 2019

British Library Cataloguing-in-Publication Data
A catalogue record for this book is available from the British Library

Library of Congress Cataloging-in-Publication Data
Names: Sunstein, Cass R., author. | Reisch, Lucia A., author.
Title: Trusting nudges: toward a bill of rights for nudging / Cass R. Sunstein and
Lucia A. Reisch.
Description: Abingdon, Oxon; New York, NY: Routledge, 2019. |
Series: Routledge advances in behavioural economics and finance |
Includes bibliographical references and index.
Subjects: LCSH: Policy sciences—Psychological aspects. | Common
good—Psychological aspects. | Decision making—Psychological aspects. |
Economics—Psychological aspects. | Public opinion.
Classification: LCC H97 (ebook) | LCC H97 .S9535 2019 (print) |
DDC 320.6—dc23
LC record available at https://lccn.loc.gov/2018043517

ISBN: 978-1-138-32278-3 (hbk)
ISBN: 978-0-367-46055-6 (pbk)

Typeset in Joanna
by codeMantra

To the memory of our fathers

CONTENTS

List of figures   viii
List of tables   ix
Preface   xi

1   Why public opinion matters   1

2   The United States, 1: Evidence   8

3   The United States, 2: Principles   19

4   Europe   29

5   A global consensus? Not quite   53

6   Trusting nudges   71

7   Educative nudges and noneducative nudges   95

8   Misconceptions   119

9   A Bill of Rights for Nudging   128

Acknowledgments   139
Index   141

FIGURES

4.1	Bar charts for information nudges: Government campaigns, total support in % (unweighted)	37
4.2	Bar charts for information nudges, governmentally mandated; total support in % (unweighted)	38
4.3	Bar charts for default rules, total support in % (unweighted)	39
4.4	Bar chart for subliminal ads, total support in % (unweighted)	40
4.5	Bar charts for other mandates	41
5.1	General information campaigns. CI, confidence interval	59
5.2	Mandatory information imposed by governments. CI, confidence interval	60
5.3	Mandatory default rules imposed by governments. CI, confidence interval	61
5.4	Mandatory subliminal advertising. CI, confidence interval	62
5.5	Mandatory choice architecture. CI, confidence interval	62
6.1	Correlation heatmap of relevant variables	76
6.2	Overall nudge approval, conditional on trust in institutions	77
6.3	Predicted marginal probabilities for approval, conditional on institutional trust	80
A6.1	Nudge approval by gender (all studies)	84
A6.2	Nudge approval among different time periods for South Korea (K), Denmark (DK), and Germany (G)	86

TABLES

2.1	American attitudes toward prominent recent nudges	10
2.2	American attitudes toward six educational campaigns	11
2.3	American attitudes toward environmental and public health nudges	12
2.4	American attitudes toward some potentially provocative nudges	13
2.5	Unpopular defaults	15
2.6	Unpopular education campaigns and disclosure	17
4.1	The 15 items of the survey	32
4.2	Overview on approval rates for the 15 nudges in the six surveyed countries	34
A4.1	Samples, sampling, and methodology	48
A4.2	Overview of political parties in the surveyed countries	49
A4.3	Clusters of the political parties in the surveyed countries	50
A4.4	Estimates of demographics and political attitude on nudge approval: Multilevel analysis	51
5.1	Estimates of selected socio-demographics and political attitude on nudge approval per nudge cluster: Multilevel analysis	64
A5.1	Observations RIM weighted/unweighted for all countries	70
6.1	Weighted OLS regression for different nudge clusters (2018 survey)	78

A6.1   Samples and sampling in the different countries (2018
       study): Types of representativeness and methodology
       (2018 survey)   87
A6.2   Descriptive statistics—all variables (2018 survey)   88
A6.3   Samples and sampling in the different countries: Types
       of representativeness and methodology (16 countries,
       all samples, all waves)   90
A6.4   Weighted OLS regression for different nudge clusters   93
7.1   Support for System 1 and System 2 nudges   102
7.2   Preference when System 1 nudge "significantly more
       effective"   103
7.3   Preference for System 1 nudges with quantitative
       information   104
7.4   Preference for System 1 nudges when System 2 nudge
       is "significantly more effective"   105
7.5   Support for System 1 and System 2 nudges by partisan
       affiliation   106
7.6   Preference when System 1 nudge "significantly more
       effective" by partisan affiliation   106
7.7   Preference with quantitative information by partisan
       affiliation   107
7.8   Preference when System 2 nudge is "significantly more
       effective" by partisan affiliation   107
7.9   Voter registration   109
7.10   Childhood obesity   110
7.11   Abortion   110
7.12   Voter registration by partisan affiliation   111
7.13   Childhood obesity by partisan affiliation   111
7.14   Abortion by partisan affiliation   111
7.15   Within-subjects results   113

PREFACE

All over the world, governments have been adopting behaviorally informed policies—policies that grow out of new findings about what human beings are actually like, and how they think and act. A growing literature examines those policies and how to make them work. But what do citizens of the world actually think about such policies? Do they approve of them? Do Russians disagree with Americans? How much, and exactly where? What are the differences among citizens of China, Japan, and South Korea? Australia and Brazil? France and Denmark? Ireland and United Kingdom? Hungary and Germany?

Over the last several years, we have been exploring these questions. We have conducted or have cooperated in nationally representative surveys in seventeen nations:

Australia	Germany	Russia
Belgium	Hungary	South Africa
Brazil	Ireland	South Korea
China	Italy	United Kingdom
Denmark	Japan	United States
France	Mexico	

The list is far from complete, of course, but it captures a significant subset of the nations of the world. As an initial step, we have narrowed and focused our efforts by asking about a set of policies that have received special attention from those interested in behavioral science in general and behavioral economics more specifically. That focus allows for some sharp comparisons and helps uncover (we think) a range of convictions about freedom, welfare, trust, and paternalism.

Those convictions tell us something about where members of the human species appear to agree with one another, and where national boundaries create significant divergences. We are also willing to speculate, a bit, about what accounts for differences within and across nations.

Ideally, of course, we would like to obtain answers to a very wide assortment of questions, involving every policy under the sun (or something close to that). We like to think that our narrower approach offers some initial clues about what would emerge from that broader inquiry. For now, we present what we have learned.

Our ultimate claim, offered by way of conclusion, involves a Bill of Rights for Nudging, one that grows directly out of empirical findings about the beliefs of citizens of numerous nations. By a Bill of Rights, we mean to suggest not judicially enforceable rights, but a set of commitments, reasonably taken to be rights, that political officials should respect. The Bill of Rights includes a ban on manipulation, respect for people's values and interests, transparency, and a prohibition on the pursuit of illicit ends. In the process of sketching that Bill of Rights, we will have something to say about human autonomy and social welfare as well.

1

WHY PUBLIC OPINION MATTERS

The last several years have seen an outpouring of work on behavioral economics, behaviorally informed policies, and "nudges," understood as interventions that steer people in particular directions but that also allow them to go their own way.[1] A reminder is a nudge ("You have a doctor's

1 See generally, e.g., Richard H. Thaler and Cass R. Sunstein, *Nudge: Improving Decisions About Health, Wealth, and Happiness* (2008) (arguing that the public's choices are influenced by small factors through the design of experiences, and that, with the knowledge of predictable psychology, nudges can help people make beneficial rational decisions); Richard H. Thaler, *Misbehaving: The Making of Behavioral Economics* (2015) (discussing various behavioral economic aspects that include endowment effects, mental accounting, consumption, self-control issues, and explains the importance of finding new methods of economic research); David Halpern, *Inside The Nudge Unit: How Small Changes Can Make a Big Difference* (2015) (showing how a policy experiment, the Behavioural Insights Team, developed small persuasive methods, nudges, that created solutions in tax, health care, crime reduction, and spurred economic growth); The World Bank, *World Development Report 2015: Mind, Society, and Behavior* (2015) (showing how the use of human psychology will force the redesigning of policies that target people's choices and actions), www.worldbank. org/content/dam/Worldbank/Publications/WDR/WDR%202015/WDR-2015-Full-Report.pdf; Pete Lunn, *Regulatory Policy and Behavioral Economics* (2014) (describing the changes of behaviorally informed politics, how they are being regulated, and finding new approaches to economic challenges); Rhys Jones et al., *Changing Behaviours: On The Rise of the Psychological State* (2013) (exploring the evolution of using the human

appointment tomorrow"). So is a warning ("Construction area"). A GPS device nudges; a default rule, specifying what happens if people do nothing, nudges. Disclosure of important information (about the risks of smoking or the costs of borrowing) counts as a nudge. Save More Tomorrow plans, allowing employees to sign up to give some portion of their future earnings to pension programs, are nudges.[2] So are Give More Tomorrow Plans, allowing employees to sign up to give some portion of their future earnings to charities.[3] A recommendation is a nudge. A criminal penalty, a civil fine, a tax, and a subsidy are not nudges, because they impose significant material incentives on people's choices. (To be sure, a very small fee or subsidy might be purely nominal and yet prove effective for behavioral reasons; if so, it might well be fair to characterize it as a nudge.)

In many nations, public officials have been drawn to nudges.[4] In 2009, the United Kingdom created a Behavioural Insights Team, focused largely on the uses of nudges, and choice architecture, to improve social outcomes; its results have been impressive.[5] Nudges play a large role in American initiatives in multiple areas, including environmental protection, financial regulation, anti-obesity policies, and education.[6] In 2014,

---

psyche to implement governing practices and challenges faced in the areas of health, finance, and the environment); Nudge, Rev. Phil. Psych. 6, 341–529 (2015) (dedicating the entirety of issue three to the topic of nudges); Riccardo Rebonato, Taking Liberties: A Critical Examination of Libertarian Paternalism (2012); Mark D. White, The Manipulation of Choice: Ethics and Libertarian Paternalism (2013). We are keenly aware that there are disputes about definitional issues and that the various sources cited here do not use the same definition. For our purposes, use of the standard definition is sufficient, and the surrounding debates need not detain us.

2 See Thaler, supra note 1, at 309–22. See generally Shlomo Benartzi, Save More Tomorrow: Practical Behavioral Finance Solutions to Improve 401(K) Plans (2012).

3 Anna Breman, Give More Tomorrow: Two Field Experiments on Altruism and Intertemporal Choice, J. Pub. Econ. 95, 1349 (2011).

4 See generally Halpern, supra note 1; Lunn, supra note 1; Jones et al., supra note 1; Cass R. Sunstein, Simpler: The Future of Government (2013); House of Lords, Science and Technology Select Committee, Behaviour Change (2011), www.publications.parliament.uk/pa/ld201012/ldselect/ldsctech/179/179.pdf.

5 See generally Halpern, supra note 1.

6 See generally Sunstein, supra note 4. For recent evidence in one domain, showing that calorie labels are having significant effects, see Partha Deb and Carmen Vargas, Who Benefits from Calorie Labeling? An Analysis of its Effects on Body Mass, 1–3 (2016) (Nat'l Bureau of Econ. Research, Working Paper No. 21992). On behaviorally informed approaches, nudges, and credit cards, see Sumit Agarwal et al., Regulating Consumer Financial Products: Evidence from Credit Cards, 16–22 (2013) (Nat'l Bureau of Econ. Research, Working Paper No. 19484).

the United States created its own Social and Behavioral Sciences Team, now called the Office of Evaluation.[7]

With an emphasis on poverty and development, the World Bank devoted its entire 2015 report to behaviorally informed tools, with a particular focus on nudging.[8] The World Bank has a Mind, Behavior, and Development Unit, focused on poverty and development. Also in 2015, President Barack Obama issued a historic Executive Order on uses of behavioral sciences in federal agencies, calling for attention to the assortment of tools standardly associated with nudging.[9] The order continues in effect. Behavioral science teams can be found in dozens of countries, including Australia, the Netherlands, France, Canada, Ireland, Germany, and Qatar. And even when formal teams are not in place, departments and ministries—and the offices of presidents, prime ministers, and chancellors—are often using behavioral insights. In fact much of the most important behaviorally informed work comes from departments and ministries, not from dedicated units of any kind.

The reason for the mounting interest should not be obscure. Nations would like to make progress on pressing social problems with tools that actually work and that do not cost a great deal. They would like to save money and lives. They would like to improve education and to reduce poverty. They would like to fuel economic growth. If governments can achieve these goals with instruments that impose minimal burdens and that preserve freedom of choice, they will take those tools extremely seriously. In domains that include savings policy,[10] climate change,[11] poverty,[12] and

---

7 Maya Shankar, *Using Behavioral Science Insights to Make Government More Effective, Simpler, and More People-Friendly*, White House Blog (February 9, 2015, 12:19 PM), www.whitehouse. gov/blog/2015/02/09/using-behavioral-science-insights-make-government-more-effective-simpler-and-more-us. William J. Congdon and Maya Shankar, The Role of Behavioral Economics in Evidence-Based Policymaking, *The Annals of the American Academy of Political and Social Sciences (AAAPS)* 678, 81–92 (2018). Article first published online: June 18, 2018; https://doi.org/10.1177/0002716218766268.

8 See The World Bank, *supra* note 1.

9 See Exec. Order No. 13707, 80 Fed. Reg. 56, 365 (Sept. 15, 2015).

10 See Thaler, *supra* note 1, at 309–22.

11 See generally Frank Beckenbach and Walter Kahlenborn, eds., *New Perspectives for Environmental Policies through Behavioral Economics* (2016); Lucia A. Reisch and John Thøgersen, eds., *Handbook of Research on Sustainable Consumption* (2015).

12 See generally Sendhil Mullainathan and Eldar Shafir, *Scarcity: Why Having Too Little Means So Much* (2013).

health care,[13] among many others, behaviorally informed approaches have attracted considerable attention, and often led to concrete reforms.

At the same time, some people have raised serious ethical concerns and objections.[14] An evident question is whether nudges should be counted as unacceptably manipulative or as an interference with freedom, rightly understood.[15] To make progress on the ethical questions, it would be possible to refer to defining commitments of various kinds—involving autonomy, dignity, welfare, and self-government—and to ask whether some, many, or all nudges run afoul of those commitments. It would also be possible to imagine cases in which nudges might have illicit goals, in which case the question would be how to identify the category of goals that count as illicit.

This is a normative task, not an empirical one. But while the normative discussions continue, it is worthwhile to ask some empirical questions. *What do people actually think about nudging and choice architecture? Do they have serious ethical objections to official nudges, or to nudges that take the form of law? Or do they believe that nudges are acceptable or desirable, even morally obligatory? Do they distinguish among nudges? What kinds of distinctions do they make?*

The answers cannot, of course, dispose of the ethical questions. The issue is how to resolve those questions in principle, and empirical findings about people's answers are not decisive. Perhaps those answers are confused, insufficiently considered, based on behavioral biases, or otherwise wrong. There is a risk that if people are responding to survey questions, they will not have time or opportunity to reflect, especially if those questions do not offer relevant facts (for example, about the costs and the benefits of the policies in question or the other policy options available). Quick answers to survey questions are not exactly the best way to obtain policy guidance.

---

13 See generally Douglas E. Hough, *Irrationality in Health Care: What Behavioral Economics Reveals About What We Do and Why* (2013).

14 The best discussion is Rebonato, *supra* note 1. See also the various contributions to Nudge, *Rev. Phil. Psych.* 6, 341–529 (2015); White, *supra* note 1; Jeremy Waldron, It's All For Your Own Good, *New York Review of Books* (October 9, 2014), www.nybooks.com/articles/archives/2014/oct/09/cass-sunstein-its-all-your-own-good. Consider in particular this question: "Deeper even than this is a prickly concern about dignity. What becomes of the self-respect we invest in our own willed actions, flawed and misguided though they often are, when so many of our choices are manipulated to promote what someone else sees (perhaps rightly) as our best interest?" *Id.* at 4. We shall have something to say about this question in Chapter 7.

15 T. M. Wilkinson, Nudging and Manipulation, *Pol. Stud.* 61, 341, 354 (2013).

Even if their answers are reflective, perhaps people do not value autonomy or dignity highly enough, or perhaps they do not quite know what those concepts mean. Perhaps people pay too little attention to social welfare,[16] or perhaps their judgments about social welfare are off the mark, at least if they are not provided with a great deal of information. We will explore the possibility that different nations, and different groups within the same nation, offer different answers, suggesting an absence of consensus.

Behavioral scientists would emphasize a related point: People's answers to ethical questions, or questions about moral approval or disapproval, might well depend on how such questions are framed. Slight differences in framing can yield dramatically different answers. Those differences are themselves a nudge; they can have major effects, and they are not easy to avoid.[17]

Here is a small example of how ethical judgments can depend on framing.[18] If people are asked whether they think that young people should be valued more than old people, they will usually say, "certainly not!" They will strenuously resist the idea that government should give a higher value to young lives than to old ones. But suppose that people are asked whether they want either (1) to save seventy people under the age of five or (2) to save seventy-five people over the age of eighty. It is reasonable to speculate (and evidence confirms) that most people will choose (1), thus demonstrating that they are willing to value a young person more than an old one.[19] It would be child's play to frame nudges so as to elicit one's preferred answer to ethical questions.

Notwithstanding these points, people's answers to carefully designed questions are interesting, because they elicit intuitions, potentially revealing patterns of thinking among those who are not required to spend a great deal of time on them. For three different reasons, they can also help to illuminate political, legal, and ethical problems. The first, and the most important, is that in democratic societies (and in nondemocratic societies as well), it is

16 See Louis Kaplow and Steven Shavell, Fairness Versus Welfare 7–8 (2006).

17 See generally Perspectives on Framing (Gideon Keren, ed., 2010).

18 See Shane Frederick, Measuring Intergenerational Time Preference: Are Future Lives Valued Less?, J. Risk and Uncertainty 256, 39, 40 (2003) (showing that people's preferences for life-saving programs depend on framing).

19 See Maureen L. Cropper et al., Preferences for Life Saving Programs: How the Public Discounts Time and Age, J. Risk and Uncertainty 8, 243, 258–59 (1994) (explaining that, while most survey respondents do not decide based only on a person's life expectancy, the fraction of people that decide to save younger people usually increases concurrently as the ratio of young to old people saved grows).

inevitable that public officials will attend to what citizens actually think. If citizens have strong ethical objections, democratic governments will hesitate before proceeding (if only because of electoral self-interest).

Such objections can operate as a kind of presumptive or de facto veto. No public official will entirely disregard a strongly felt moral concern on the part of significant segments of the public. And if people do not have moral objections, and if they welcome nudges as helpful and desirable, public officials will be attentive to their views. Widespread public approval can operate as a license or a permission slip, or perhaps as a spur or a prod.[20] Similar points hold in nondemocratic nations, where public officials know that they can learn from what citizens think, and where they are keenly aware that their power might depend on listening to them and considering their concerns.

The second reason is epistemic: People's judgments provide relevant information about how to think about the ethical issues even if that information is not conclusive. It is not necessary to make strong claims about the "wisdom of crowds," especially on contested ethical issues, in order to believe that an ethical judgment on the part of those who might be subject to nudges deserves respectful attention. Public officials should be humble and attentive to the views of others, and if strong majorities favor or oppose nudges, their views are entitled to consideration. We do not mean to suggest that public approval or disapproval in a survey setting should dispose of ethical (or other) issues. Reflection, deliberation, expertise, and information greatly matter (see Chapter 9). But public reactions deserve attention.

The third reason involves the commitment to democratic self-government. If that commitment matters, officials should pay attention to what people think, even if they disagree. To be sure, people's considered judgments might diverge from what emerges from brief surveys. Their considered judgments deserve priority. And if public officials have a clear sense that an approach or a nudge would reduce social welfare, there is a strong argument that they should not adopt that approach or nudge even if people would like them to do so—just as there is a strong argument that they should adopt an approach that increases social welfare even if people oppose it. Individual rights and

---

20 We are bracketing here questions about interest-group dynamics and coalition formation, which can of course complicate official judgments. Politicians are interested in many things that bear on reelection, not merely the views of the median voter. And of course, there are important differences between the legislative and executive branches on this count, with the latter frequently having more "space" for technocratic judgment.

private autonomy also have their claims, whatever majorities may think. We shall explore these points in Chapter 9. But when public officials are uncertain about whether an approach is desirable, it is reasonable, in the name of self-government, for them to give consideration to the views of members of the public.

As we shall see, current research in many nations supports a single conclusion: At least in general, the majority of citizens of most nations have no views, either positive or negative, about nudging in general; *their assessment turns on whether they approve of the purposes and effects of particular nudges*. As we shall see, strong majorities in diverse nations tend to be supportive of nudges of the kind that have been seriously proposed, or acted on, by actual institutions in recent years.

With some qualifications, this enthusiasm extends across standard partisan lines; perhaps surprisingly, it unifies people with diverse political convictions. So long as people believe that the goal is both legitimate and important, they are likely to favor nudges in its direction. When there is disagreement, it is usually because of differences about the legitimacy and the importance of the goal of the particular nudge. This is an important finding, because it suggests that most people do not share the concern that nudges, as such, should be taken as manipulative or as an objectionable interference with autonomy. Some preliminary evidence suggests that people are far more negative about mandates and bans, even when they are taken to have perfectly legitimate ends; many people do care about freedom of choice as such, and they will reject many well-motivated policies that do not allow for it.

To summarize the story that we shall tell here: People are most likely to oppose those nudges that (1) promote what they see as illicit goals or (2) are perceived as inconsistent with either the interests or values of most choosers. A more particular finding, one that counts against some default rules, is that people *do not want policymakers to produce economic or other losses by using people's inertia or inattention against them*. In addition, people tend to prefer nudges that target deliberative processes to those that target unconscious or subconscious processes, and may react against the latter—though they do not by any means rule the latter out of bounds and will often approve of them as well. When the political valence of nudging is clear, their evaluation of nudges much turns on that valence, which reinforces the general view that in most cases, it is people's assessment of the ends of particular nudges, rather than of nudging as such, that settles their judgments.

Now for the details.

2

THE UNITED STATES, 1: EVIDENCE

To test public opinion in the United States, we devised a nationally representative survey involving thirty-four nudges. The survey was administered in 2016 by Survey Sampling International and included 563 Americans, with a margin of error of plus or minus 4.1 percentage points. People were asked simply whether they approved or disapproved of the relevant nudges.

From their responses, two dominant principles emerge. *First*, Americans reject nudges that promote what they see as illicit ends (such as religious or political favoritism). *Second*, Americans reject nudges that they view as inconsistent with the interests or values of most choosers. By contrast, there is widespread support for nudges that are taken to have legitimate ends and to be consistent with the interests and the values of most choosers.

We shall turn to other nations in due course, but in the United States, at least, it follows that numerous nudges—default rules, warnings, and public education campaigns—are likely to attract bipartisan support, so long as people approve of their ends and think that they are consistent with choosers' values and interests. Several of the policies tested here can be counted as highly tendentious and arguably manipulative. Nonetheless, they attracted majority support, with the single (and highly exotic) exception of subliminal advertising (which, surprisingly, receives substantial minority support in the context of efforts to combat smoking and overeating). It follows that Americans are reluctant to reject nudges as unacceptably manipulative.[1] Their evaluations are dominated by their assessment of the legitimacy of the underlying ends.[2]

As we will see, political divisions sometimes affect the level of support; Democrats are more favorably disposed toward certain health and safety nudges than are Republicans. In cases that raise strong partisan differences, such divisions will map onto nudges as well. It is easy to imagine nudges that Republicans would support more strongly than would Democrats—for example, nudges to discourage abortion or religious instruction. But across a wide range, clear majorities of Democrats and Republicans (and also independents) are in full agreement about what they support and what they reject.

Popular nudges

In recent years, the US government has adopted or promoted a large number of nudges. Three of the most prominent include: (1) mandatory calorie labels at chain restaurants; (2) mandatory graphic warnings on cigarette packages[3] (struck down by a federal court of appeals[4]); and (3) automatic enrollment in savings plans, subject to opt out.[5] The nation-

---

1   Notably, Janice Jung and Barbara Mellers, American Attitudes Towards Nudges, *Judgement and Decision Making* 11, 62 (2016) find that people reject this nudge as manipulative: "Use of increasingly narrower white lines on roadways that create the visual illusions of speeding up to control vehicle speeding." *Id.* at 66. This nudge might be taken to fall in the same category as subliminal advertising because it is taken to fall right on the line between manipulation and deception.

2   To be sure, provision of information about the consequences of nudges might unsettle some of people's responses, and perhaps move people in the direction of what follows from an all-things-considered welfare assessment. If so, any such movements would be consistent with the general claim here; they would merely reflect a more informed judgment about what ends would, in fact, be promoted by nudges. For example, people might be less enthusiastic about compulsory disclosure of uses of GMOs if they were convinced that such disclosure did not provide useful information and might mislead people. We shall have something to say about this question in later chapters.

3   See Cigarette Package and Advertising Warnings: Required Warnings, 21 C.F.R. § 1141.10 (2015).

4   On the FDA's effort to require graphic warnings on packages, *see* R.J. Reynolds *Tobacco Co. v. FDA*, 823 F. Supp. 2d 36 (D.D.C. 2011), *aff'd on other grounds*, 696 F.3d 1205 (D.C. Cir. 2012).

5   For discussion of relevant laws and policies, see generally *Automatic: Changing the Way America Saves* (William G. Gale et al., eds., 2009).

Table 2.1 American attitudes toward prominent recent nudges

	Calorie labels	*Graphic warn-ings (cigarettes)*	*Federal encouragement: Auto-enrollment*	*Federal mandate: Auto-enrollment*
Total support (approval/ disapproval in percentages)	87/13	74/26	80/20	71/29
Democrats	92/8	77/23	88/12	78/22
Independents	88/12	74/26	75/25	67/33
Republicans	77/23	68/32	73/27	62/38

ally representative sample found substantial majority support for all three policies, including support for (3) regardless of whether it consists of federal "encouragement" of such enrollment or a federal mandate for automatic enrollment, imposed on large employers (see Table 2.1).

About 87 percent of Americans favored calorie labels and 74 percent favored graphic warnings.[6] Both policies had strong majority support from Democrats, Republicans, and independents. Overall, 80 percent and 71 percent respectively approved of encouraged and mandatory enrollment in savings plans. Here as well, all three groups showed strong majority support.[7]

Three educational campaigns also attracted widespread approval (see Table 2.2). Respondents were overwhelmingly supportive of a public education campaign from the federal government to combat childhood obesity (82 percent approval, again with strong support from Democrats, Republicans, and independents). Similarly, they were highly supportive of a public education campaign from the federal government designed to combat distracted driving, with graphic stories and images (85 percent approval). About 75 percent of people favored a federal education campaign to encourage people not to discriminate on the basis of sexual orientation, though here there was a noteworthy division across party lines—85 percent of Democrats, 57 percent of Republicans, and 75 percent of independents.

---

6 Note that there were statistically significant differences with respect to calorie labels between Republicans (77 percent approval) and both Democrats (92 percent approval) and independents (88 percent approval).

7 Here as well, there were statistically significant differences between Democrats and Republicans for both policies and between Democrats and independents with respect to encouragement (Encouraged: 88 percent of Democrats, 73 percent of Republicans, and 75 percent of independents. Mandated: 78 percent of Democrats, 62 percent of Republicans, and 67 percent of independents).

Table 2.2 American attitudes toward six educational campaigns[8]

	Childhood obesity	Distracted driving	Sexual orientation discrimination	Movie theaters	Animal Welfare Society	Obesity (arguably manipulative)
Total support (approval/ disapproval in percentages)	82/18	85/15	75/25	53/47	52/48	57/43
Democrats	90/11	88/12	85/15	61/39	59/41	61/40
Independents	81/19	84/16	75/25	51/49	55/45	60/40
Republicans	70/30	80/20	57/43	41/59	34/66	47/53

Three other educational campaigns attracted majority support, but at significantly lower levels and with only minority approval from Republicans. About 53 percent of Americans favored a federal requirement that movie theaters run public education messages to discourage people from smoking and overeating. Democrats showed higher approval ratings than Republicans (61 percent as opposed to 41 percent, with independents at 51 percent). By a very small majority (52 percent), Americans supported a public education campaign, by the federal government itself, to encourage people to give money to the Animal Welfare Society of America (a hypothetical organization) (59 percent of Democrats, 34 percent of Republicans, and 55 percent of independents; party was a statistically significant factor). This latter finding seems surprising; it could not easily be predicted that respondents would want their government to design a campaign to promote donations to an animal welfare society.

About 57 percent of people supported an aggressive public education campaign from the federal government to combat obesity, showing obese children struggling to exercise and also showing interviews with obese adults, who are saying such things as, "My biggest regret in life is that I have not managed to control my weight," and "To me, obesity is like a terrible curse." This question was designed to test people's reactions to a tendentious and arguably manipulative campaign, which might have been expected to receive widespread disapproval, but it did not. Indeed, one of the goals of the question was to establish such disapproval—but it was not found here. Here, there was a significant disparity between Democrats

8 Percentages may not total 100 due to rounding.

(61 percent approval) and independents (60 percent approval) on the one hand and Republicans on the other (47 percent approval); the difference between the views of Democrats and those of Republicans was statistically significant.

Most Americans were also supportive of multiple efforts to use choice architecture to promote public health and environmental protection (see Table 2.3). In recent years, there has been considerable international discussion of "traffic lights" systems for food, which would use the familiar red, yellow, and green to demarcate health rankings.[9] In the United States, the national government has shown no official interest in these initiatives, but with respondents in the nationally representative survey, the idea attracted strong support (64 percent). There was also majority approval of automatic use of "green" energy providers, subject to opt out[10]—perhaps surprisingly, with support for automatic use of green energy whether it consisted of federal "encouragement" (72 percent) or instead a federal mandate on large electricity providers (67 percent).[11] In these cases, there were significant differences across partisan lines, but majorities of Democrats, Republicans, and independents were all supportive.

Table 2.3 American attitudes toward environmental and public health nudges

	GMO labels	Salt labels	Healthy food placement	Traffic lights	Organ donor choice	Encouragement: Green energy	Mandate: Green energy
Total support (in percentages)	86/14	73/27	56/44	64/36	70/30	72/28	67/33
Democrats	89/11	79/21	63/37	71/29	75/25	82/18	79/21
Independents	87/13	72/28	57/43	61/39	69/31	66/34	63/37
Republicans	80/20	61/39	43/57	57/43	62/38	61/39	51/49

9 See Anne N. Thorndike et al., Traffic-Light Labels and Choice Architecture: Promoting Healthy Food Choices, Am. J. Preventive Med. 46, 143, 143–44 (2014).

10 See Cass R. Sunstein and Lucia A. Reisch, Automatically Green: Behavioral Economics and Environmental Protection, Harv. Envtl. L. Rev. 38, 127, 134–35 (2014).

11 On the difficulty of this question, see id. at 155–57.

Table 2.4 American attitudes toward some potentially provocative nudges[12]

	Listing incumbent politician first	Automatic voter registration	Husband's last name	Mandatory manufacturing label: Labor violations	Mandatory manufacturing label: Aiding terrorists
Total support (in percentages)	53/47	53/47	58/42	60/40	54/46
Democrats	58/42	63/37	61/40	67/33	56/44
Independents	51/49	50/50	56/44	57/43	49/51
Republicans	47/53	39/61	57/43	50/50	58/42

Most respondents were in favor of requiring companies to disclose whether the food they sell contains genetically modified organisms (GMOs) (86 percent approval). There was strong majority support (73 percent) for a mandatory warning label on products that have unusually high levels of salt, as in, "This product has been found to contain unusually high levels of salt, which may be harmful to your health." Perhaps surprisingly, most respondents (but not most Republicans) approved of a state requirement that grocery stores put their most healthy foods in prominent, visible locations (56 percent approval: 63 percent from Democrats, 43 percent from Republicans, 57 percent from independents). Respondents also supported a state requirement that people must say, when they obtain their driver's license, whether they want to be organ donors (70 percent approval: 75 percent from Democrats, 62 percent from Republicans, 69 percent from independents).[13] For all of these policies, the differences between Democrats and Republicans were statistically significant.

Five other forms of choice architecture, which might be expected to be far more controversial, nonetheless obtained majority support (see Table 2.4). The first would list the name of the incumbent politician first, on every ballot. It might be expected that this pro-incumbent nudge would be widely rejected, because respondents might not want the voting process

12 Percentages may not total 100 due to rounding.
13 Another study, discussed below, finds that most Americans reject a default rule to the effect that people would be presumed to be organ donors, subject to opt out. *See* William Hagman et al., Public Views on Policies Involving Nudges, *Rev. Phil. and Psychol.* 6, 439, 446 (2015).

to be skewed in favor of incumbents and because any effort to enlist order effects might be seen as manipulative (as indeed it should be). But a bare majority (53 percent) approved of this approach, perhaps because most people believed that it would promote clarity, perhaps because they did not see the risk of bias from order effects.

There was also majority approval (53 percent) for the approach, adopted in several American states such as Oregon and in the majority of European nations, of automatically registering eligible citizens as voters, subject to opt out. Interestingly, most Republicans (61 percent) rejected this approach. One reason might be that they believe that people who do not take the time to register to vote ought not to be counted as voters. Another reason is that they might believe that Oregon's approach would favor Democrats. Yet another reason is that they might believe that such an approach would increase the risk of fraud.

By a modest majority, most people (58 percent) also approved of an approach by which women's last names would automatically be changed to that of their husband, subject to opt out. This approach obtained majority support from Democrats, Republicans, and independents. This result is especially noteworthy in view of the fact that an approach to this effect would almost certainly be unconstitutional as a form of sex discrimination, even if it tracked behavior and preferences.[14] We might expect a difference between men and women on this question, but notably, 58 percent of both groups approved of this approach.

Finally, there was majority support for a federal labeling requirement for products that come from companies that have repeatedly violated the nation's labor laws (such as laws requiring occupational safety or forbidding discrimination). About 60 percent of participants supported that policy, with a significant difference between Democrats (67 percent approval) and Republicans (50 percent approval). There was also majority support for federally required labels on products that come from countries that have recently harbored terrorists. This approach attracted 54 percent approval—56 percent from Democrats, 58 percent from Republicans, and 49 percent from independents.

---

14 See *Craig v. Boren*, 429 US 190, 200–4 (1976) (finding Oklahoma's statute permitting females over the age of eighteen to buy 3.2 percent beer but prohibiting males under the age of twenty-one from buying the same beer "invidiously discriminates against males 18–20 years old"). For valuable discussion of the general topic, see Elizabeth F. Emens, Changing Name Changing: Framing Rules and the Future of Marital Names, *U. Chi. L. Rev.* 74, 761, 772–74 (2007).

Unpopular nudges

By contrast, twelve nudges were widely disapproved. Of these, seven involved uses of default rules (see Table 2.5). Two of these defaults were designed so as to be not merely provocative but also highly offensive, in the sense of being violative of widely held principles of neutrality, and strong majorities took them exactly as they were designed.

Under the first, a state would assume that people want to register as Democrats, subject to opt out if people explicitly say that they want to register as Republicans or independents. Of course, a default rule of this kind should be taken as an effort to skew the political process (and it would certainly be unconstitutional for that reason).[15] The overwhelming majority of people, including three-quarters of Democrats, rejected this approach (26 percent total approval: 32 percent of Democrats, 16 percent of Republicans, and 26 percent of independents, with statistically significant differences between Democrats and Republicans). The second was a state law assuming that people are Christian, for purposes of the census,

Table 2.5 Unpopular defaults

	Democrat registration	Christian on census	Wife's last name	Red Cross	Animal Welfare Society	United Way	Carbon emissions charge
Total support (in percentages)	26/74	21/79	24/76	27/73	26/74	24/76	36/64
Democrats	32/68	22/78	28/72	30/70	30/70	26/74	43/57
Independents	26/74	17/83	23/77	28/72	25/75	25/75	34/66
Republicans	16/84	27/73	18/82	20/80	20/80	17/83	25/75

15 In principle, the problem would be most interesting in an area in which the default rule tracked reality. If most people are, in fact, Democrats, is it clearly objectionable if a city or state assumes that they are for purposes of registration? The answer is almost certainly yes; political affiliations should be actively chosen, not assumed by government. This principle almost certainly has constitutional foundations (though it has not been tested): If a voting district consisted of 80 percent Democratic voters, it would not be acceptable to assume that all voters intend to register as Democrats. But we are aware that this brief comment does not give anything like an adequate answer to some complex questions about the use of "mass" default rules that track majority preferences and values. For discussion, see Cass R. Sunstein, *Choosing Not To Choose: Understanding the Value of Choice* 77 (2015).

unless they specifically state otherwise. Such a default rule could also be seen as an attempt to push religious affiliations in preferred directions (and it would similarly be unconstitutional).[16] Here too, there was widespread disapproval (21 percent overall approval: 22 percent of Democrats, 27 percent of Republicans, and 17 percent of independents).

The third unpopular default rule (completing the set of unconstitutional nudges) involved a state law assuming that upon marriage, husbands would automatically change their last names to that of their wives, subject to opt out (24 percent total approval: 28 percent of Democrats, 18 percent of Republicans, and 23 percent of independents). Interestingly, there was no gender disparity here (just as with the question that involved the opposite defaults); 24 percent of both men and women approved. With the fourth, the federal government would assume, on tax returns, that people want to donate fifty dollars to the Red Cross, subject to opt out if people explicitly say that they do not want to make that donation (27 percent approval: 30 percent of Democrats, 20 percent of Republicans, 28 percent of independents). The fifth was identical but substituted the Animal Welfare Society for the Red Cross. Not surprisingly, that question also produced widespread disapproval (26 percent approval: 30 percent of Democrats, 20 percent of Republicans, and 25 percent of independents). Somewhat surprisingly, and revealingly, the numbers were essentially the same for the two charities, even though it might be expected that presumed donations for the Red Cross would be more popular.

With the sixth, state government assumed that state employees would give twenty dollars per month to the United Way, a large US charity, subject to opt out. It might be expected that because state government and state employees were involved, approval rates might grow. But they did not (24 percent approval: 26 percent of Democrats, 17 percent of Republicans, and 25 percent of independents). With the seventh, a majority (64 percent) disapproved of a federal requirement that airlines charge people, with their airline tickets, a specific amount to offset their carbon emissions (about ten dollars per ticket), subject to opt out if passengers

---

16 Here as well we could imagine interesting questions if the default rule tracked reality. If most people in a city or state are Christians, is it so clearly illegitimate to presume, for purposes of the census, that most people are Christians, subject to opt out? But with respect to religion, as with respect to politics, there is a strong social and constitutional norm in favor of official neutrality, which would be violated even if a particular default reflected majority preferences and values.

said that they did not want to pay. Interestingly, a strong majority of Democrats (57 percent) disapproved of this approach, although the number for Republicans was significantly higher (75 percent).

The five other unpopular nudges involved information and education (see Table 2.6). With the first (and most extreme), a newly elected president adopted a public education campaign designed to convince people that criticism of his decisions is unpatriotic and potentially damaging to national security. There was overwhelming disapproval of this campaign (23 percent approval: 24 percent of Democrats, 21 percent of Republicans, and 22 percent of independents). What is perhaps most noteworthy here is not majority disapproval, but the fact that over one-fifth of Americans, on essentially a nonpartisan basis, were in favor of this most unusual public campaign.

With the second, the federal government adopted a public education campaign designed to convince mothers to stay home to take care of their young children. Over two-thirds of respondents rejected this nudge (33 percent approval: 33 percent of Democrats, 31 percent of Republicans, and 34 percent of independents). The third involved a government requirement that movie theaters run subliminal advertisements to discourage smoking and overeating. Here too, there was majority disapproval (41 percent approval: 47 percent of Democrats, 42 percent of Republicans, and 35 percent of independents). It is noteworthy and surprising, however, that over two-fifths of people actually supported this requirement.

Table 2.6 Unpopular education campaigns and disclosure[17]

	Unpatriotic criticism	Stay-at-home mothers	Subliminal advertising	Mandatory manufacturing label: Communism	Transgender
Total support (in percentages)	23/77	33/67	41/59	44/56	41/59
Democrats	24/76	33/67	47/53	47/53	49/51
Independents	22/78	34/67	35/65	42/58	38/62
Republicans	21/79	31/69	42/58	43/57	29/71

17 Percentages may not total 100 due to rounding.

With the fourth, the federal government would require all products that come from a Communist country (such as China or Cuba) to be sold with the label "Made in whole or in part under Communism." Slightly over half of respondents disapproved of this requirement (44 percent approval: 47 percent of Democrats, 43 percent of Republicans, and 42 percent of independents). With the fifth, a majority (59 percent) also rejected a public education campaign from the federal government, informing people that it is possible for people to change their gender from male to female or from female to male and encouraging people to consider that possibility "if that is really what they want to do." There is yet another surprise here: this somewhat adventurous campaign was endorsed by 41 percent of respondents; note that approval rates differed between Democrats (49 percent), Republicans (29 percent), and independents (38 percent).

3

THE UNITED STATES, 2: PRINCIPLES

What separates the approved nudges from the rejected ones? Two principles seem to dominate the cases. First, Americans *reject nudges that they take to have illegitimate goals*. In a self-governing society, for example, it is illegitimate to attempt to convince people that criticism of a public official is unpatriotic. At least in the United States, nudges that favor a particular religion or political party will meet with widespread disapproval, even among people of that very religion or party.[1] This simple principle justifies a prediction: Whenever people think that the motivations of the choice architect are illicit, they will disapprove of the nudge.

---

1 We could, of course, imagine a nation in which favoritism on the basis of religion or party would attract widespread support and might be seen as analogous to a default rule in which women's last name changes to that of their husband (which is approved, it will be recalled, by a majority of respondents here). In such a nation, a default rule in favor of the most popular party, or the dominant religion, might be taken to track people's preferences and values, and not to be a violation of the governing conception of neutrality at all.

To be sure, that prediction might not seem terribly surprising, but it suggests an important point, which is that people will not oppose (for example) default rules and warnings as such; everything will turn on what they are nudging people *toward*. By contrast, mandates do run into some opposition simply because they are mandates. When there are partisan differences in judgments about nudges, it is often because of partisan disagreement about whether the relevant motivations are legitimate. Resolution of such disagreements would of course depend on judgments having nothing to do with nudging as such.

Second, Americans oppose nudges *that they perceive as inconsistent with the interests or values of most choosers*. The most direct evidence is the finding that while most Americans support automatic name change for women, they reject automatic name change for men. The evident reason is that the former tracks people's interests and values (at least in general), while the latter countermands them.[2] Any default rule, of course, is likely to harm at least some people; some people will want, for good reason, to opt out, and some people who want to opt out will not do so, perhaps because of inertia and procrastination. This point is a potential objection to default rules in general.

By itself, however, that fact is not enough to produce public opprobrium. Recall that there is majority approval for automatic voter registration and automatic enrollment in pension plans and green energy, apparently because respondents think that those nudges are in most people's interests.[3] Recall too that most respondents are favorably disposed toward public education campaigns designed to combat obesity and discrimination on the basis of sexual orientation. By contrast, most people oppose public education campaigns

2 Here as well, we could easily imagine a population that would reverse these results. Suppose that one believes that automatically assuming that wives take their husbands' last names undermines sex equality, and automatically assuming that husbands take their wives' last names promotes sex equality. For those who have these beliefs, and are committed to sex equality, reversing the majority's views might seem attractive.

3 Note, however, that savings defaults are importantly different from green defaults. The former are adopted because they are in the interest of choosers; money that would go to take-home pay goes into savings, and so choosers do not lose anything on net (while also saving for retirement). The latter are adopted because they help to solve a collective action problem. With respect to green defaults, the question did not specify whether people would have to pay for green energy. Not surprisingly, people are more likely to opt out if they would. *See* Simon Hedlin and Cass R. Sunstein, *Does Active Choosing Promote Green Energy Use? Experimental Evidence* (Mossavar-Rahmani Ctr. for Bus. and Gov't Reg. Pol'y Program, Working Paper RPP-2015-13, 2015).

to encourage women to stay at home and to inform people that they can change their gender, apparently on the ground that those campaigns are inconsistent with what people regard as prevailing interests and values.[4]

When people are deciding whether to favor default rules, the size of the group of disadvantaged people undoubtedly matters. If a default rule harms a majority, it is unlikely to have much appeal. If the disadvantaged group is large (but not a majority), people might reject a default rule and favor active choosing instead. The precise nature of this principle remains to be tested, but most respondents appear to accept an important third principle: *Before certain losses can occur, people must affirmatively express their wishes.* The principle forbids the state from taking certain goods by default.[5]

It is relevant here that most respondents favor a state requirement that when obtaining their driver's license, people indicate whether they want to be organ donors (and thus favor active choosing), even though most Americans reject a default rule in favor of being an organ donor. The apparent idea involves the central importance of individual consent. Without that consent, the government may not take things that people currently have. The boundaries of this principle remain to be specified. People are willing to approve of automatic enrollment if it will protect their future selves (as in the case of pensions) and also if it will protect the environment. Most people do not oppose the tax system as such. But "takings" seem to raise a red flag.

---

4 To be sure, there is an ambiguity in these findings. Do respondents reject nudges that are (a) inconsistent with their *own* interests or values or (b) inconsistent with the interests or values of *most choosers*? On this question, the findings here do not provide a clear test. When respondents reject nudges, they probably believe that the nudges that are inconsistent with their own interests or values are also inconsistent with the interests or values of most choosers. It would be interesting and possible to pose questions that would enable us to choose between (a) and (b). Consider here the important finding that when a nudge is said to be targeted at "you," people are less likely to support it than when it is said to be targeted at "people in general." James F. M. Cornwell and David H. Krantz, Public Policy for Thee, But Not for Me: Varying the Grammatical Person of Public Policy Justifications Influences Their Support, *Judgement and Decision Making* 5, 433 (2014). Our own study implicitly assumes the "people in general" frame.

5 Whether this principle is triggered will depend on a theory of entitlement, from which any account of "losses" will flow. In the questions here, that issue is not especially complicated. If a default rule will ensure that people give money to specified charities (subject to opt out), it will impose a loss. But we could imagine harder cases—as, for example, with adjustments in the social security program where losses and gains might not be self-evident and might be subject to framing.

Note in this regard that strong majorities of people reject automatic charitable donations of diverse kinds. The apparent concern is that, as a result of inertia, procrastination, or inattention, people might find themselves giving money to a charity even though they do not wish to do so. We might therefore complement the third principle with a fourth and narrower one, which can be seen as a specification: *Most people reject automatic enrollment in charitable giving programs, at least if they are operated by public institutions.* Though it does not involve money, the case of carbon offsets can be understood in similar terms; while it does not involve a charitable donation and instead might be seen as an effort to prevent a harmful act, Americans appear to want active consent. As noted, we do not yet know the exact limits of apparent public skepticism about default rules that would give away people's money without their active consent, but there is no doubt that such skepticism exists.

We have seen that people generally favor disclosures that, in their view, bear on health, safety, or the environment (salt content, GMOs). At the same time, the results leave open the question whether and when people will favor mandatory disclosures that involve political issues associated with production of a product rather than the health and environmental effects of the product itself. Americans seem closely divided on that question. With repeated violations of the nation's labor laws, and nations that harbor terrorism, such disclosure achieved majority support—but not with products coming from Communist nations. Americans might well demand a certain threshold of egregiousness, in terms of the behavior of those who produce a good or service, before they will want to require disclosure of that behavior. On this question, partisan differences are to be expected because people will disagree about whether the relevant threshold has been met, and about what it exactly is.

It is tempting, and not inconsistent with the data, to suggest that reactions to nudges also show the influence of a fifth principle: *Americans reject nudges that they regard as unacceptably manipulative.* The subliminal advertising finding can be taken as support for this principle. But what counts as unacceptable manipulation?[6] Most Americans are in favor of graphic warning labels on cigarettes; they like default rules (if consistent with people's values and interests); a majority favors a mandatory cafeteria design to promote healthy eating; people approve of a graphic campaign to discourage

6 See Jung and Mellers, *supra* note 21, at 66–68 (finding public disapproval of visual illusion designed to promote safety on the highways).

distracted driving; with respect to obesity, a majority favors a somewhat tendentious public education, one that could plausibly be characterized as manipulative. No one likes manipulation in the abstract, but there do not appear to be many cases in which people are willing to reject nudges as unacceptably manipulative, at least if they have legitimate ends and are taken to be in the interest of most choosers.

Partisanship

What is the role of partisan differences? Democrats and Republicans will sometimes disagree, of course, about whether the goals of a particular nudge are illicit, and they will also disagree, on occasion, about whether a nudge is consistent with the interests or values of choosers. For example, those who disapprove of abortion will be especially likely to support nudges that are designed to discourage abortion; those who do not disapprove of abortion will be unlikely to support such nudges. Imagine an anti-abortion nudge in the form of a law requiring pregnant women seeking abortions to be presented with a fetal heartbeat or a sonogram. We can predict, with a high degree of confidence, that Democrats would show lower approval ratings than Republicans. Our own study on Amazon's Mechanical Turk finds exactly that: only about 28 percent of Democrats approve, while 70 percent of Republicans do so.[7] With respect to a public education campaign informing people that they can change genders, the significant difference between Democrats and Republicans should not exactly come as a big surprise.

But there is another and more general division as well. Even when majorities of Democrats, Republicans, and independents support a particular initiative, the level of support is sometimes higher within one group than within another. Even if the underlying end is broadly shared—as it is, for example, in the area of public health—some subset of Republicans sometimes seems skeptical of government nudges, taken as such, and will *therefore disapprove of them even if they do accept the legitimacy of the end and do not think that the nudge is inconsistent with choosers' interests or values.* Some Republicans, and undoubtedly some Democrats and independents, appear to support another

---

7 The survey and the results are available from the authors on request. The precise question asked people whether they approve or disapprove of a "state requirement that pregnant women must see a sonogram of their fetus, and hear its heartbeat, before proceeding to have an abortion." Interestingly, only about one-third of independents approved, essentially the same as Democrats.

principle: *There should be a rebuttable presumption against nudging, at least if the government can avoid it.*

Most Americans reject this principle, and the survey does not provide conclusive evidence that significant numbers embrace it, but it is highly suggestive. Many people reject graphic health warnings on cigarette packages (26 percent), an educational campaign for childhood obesity (18 percent), an educational campaign for distracted driving (15 percent), and a traffic lights system for food (36 percent). It is reasonable to infer that those who oppose such nudges agree that they have legitimate ends and are in the interest of most choosers—but nonetheless do not favor government intervention.

It is important to see that the strength and domain of any anti-nudge presumption will vary with the particular issue, with partisan affiliations, and with competing views about the role of government. In some of the cases, Republicans are more skeptical of nudges than are Democrats. With calorie labels and childhood obesity campaigns, for example, there are significant differences in the levels of support within the two groups, even though majorities of both are supportive. But in some cases, Republicans are undoubtedly more enthusiastic about nudges than are Democrats, as in the case of the anti-abortion nudge. The fact that few such cases are found here is an artifact of the particular questions. If the issue involved automatic enrollment in programs by which high-income earners automatically receive capital gains tax benefits, for example, we can predict, with some confidence, that Republicans would be more supportive than Democrats. Evidence supports that prediction.[8]

Nudges vs. mandates

We have suggested that many Americans are skeptical of certain mandates, even if they have legitimate ends. To test that proposition, we used Amazon's Mechanical Turk (with 309 participants) to test American reactions to three pairs of initiatives. The initiatives involved savings (with a 3 percent contribution rate), safe sex education, and education about intelligent design. In all cases, the nudge was far more popular than the mandate (and received majority support), and indeed, in all cases, the mandate ran into majority disapproval. So long as people could opt out, the savings initiative received

8 See Id.

69 percent approval; safe sex education, 77 percent; and intelligent design, 56 percent. As mandates, the three fell to approval rates of 19 percent, 43 percent, and 24 percent respectively.

Consistent with other findings, it follows that most Americans do oppose certain kinds of mandates as such, even when they are enthusiastic about the underlying ends and are supportive of nudges that are designed to promote those ends. We have seen that majorities of Americans have no general view about nudges as such; their assessments turn on the principles outlined here. With mandates, many Americans do have a general view, and it is not favorable. Of course it is also true that Americans do support mandates of various kinds, especially when harm to others is involved (as in the case of the criminal law and many regulatory requirements). In that light, we do not mean to suggest that Americans oppose mandates as such. That proposition would be too broad. The only point is that they oppose mandates even when they approve of their goals—and that they do approve interventions that preserve freedom of choice.

Partisan nudge bias

Do political judgments matter to people's assessment of nudges? Our survey of Americans finds some support for an affirmative answer, in the sense that Republicans are less likely to approve of certain nudges than Democrats are. As we have also noted, Republicans are *more* likely to approve of certain nudges than Democrats are. Casual observation suggests a broader possibility: When a particular administration uses behaviorally informed tools, those who are inclined to oppose that administration are not likely to love those tools. Consider this hypothesis: *At least across a wide range, people have no considered view on nudges as such. Their evaluations turn on whether they approve of the politics of the particular nudge, or the particular nudges that come to mind.*

More specific evidence supports this view. In a series of studies, David Tannenbaum, Craig Fox, and Todd Rogers have found what they call "partisan nudge bias."[9] Focusing on policies favoring automatic enrollment in pension plans, they randomly assigned people to conditions in which they learned that such policies had been implemented by the Bush

---

9 David Tannenbaum et al., On the Misplaced Politics of Behavioural Policy Interventions, *Nature Human Behaviour* 1(0130) (2017), at 1–7 (suggesting that powerful behavioral insights can allow for a tendency to gravitate towards default options).

Administration, the Obama Administration, or an unnamed Administration. After informing participants about the policy nudge, Tannenbaum et al. specifically reminded them that defaults could be used "across a wide range of policies beyond the illustration above" and asked how they felt, setting the particular application aside, "about actively setting default options as a general approach to public policy."[10]

The basic finding was that on the *general* question, people were much influenced by whether Bush or Obama was responsible for the particular nudge that they read about. When participants were informed that the pension default had been implemented by Obama, liberals tended to display relative support for the use of defaults as a general policy tool, whereas conservatives tended to oppose them. But when told that the same policy had been implemented by Bush, that pattern was eliminated; liberals displayed relative opposition to the use of defaults, whereas conservatives supported them.

Tannenbaum et al. also asked respondents about a series of nudges that had an identifiable political valence, immediately triggering disparate reactions from liberals and conservatives. These included increasing participation by low-income individuals in existing food stamp and supplemental nutrition assistance programs (liberal valence); increasing claims by high-income individuals for existing capital gains tax breaks (conservative valence); increasing participation in safe sex and effective contraception use educational programs for high-school children (liberal valence); increasing participation in intelligent design educational programs for high-school children (conservative valence); and a generic, context-free policy illustration (no valence). There were five different types of policy nudges: (1) automatic enrollment defaults, (2) implementation intentions, (3) public commitments, (4) highlighting losses, and (5) descriptive social norms. As in their first study, Tannenbaum et al. asked people about their *general* views about nudges after seeing the relevant example. Participants were specifically reminded that the approach was general and could be used across a wide range of policies.

The result was unambiguous: People are significantly more likely to approve of nudges in general when they favor the particular political objectives used to illustrate them. When the nudges were applied to traditionally liberal policies (food stamps, safe sex), liberals were relatively supportive

10 *Id.*

of nudges as policy tools, while conservatives were relatively opposed to their general use. This pattern reversed when those same nudges were applied to traditionally conservative policy goals (capital gains programs, intelligent design education programs).

Interestingly, and importantly, when nudges were attached to a *generic* policy objective, there was no association between political orientation and people's evaluation of nudges; apparently, conservatives and liberals do not disagree on the general question. A particularly striking finding is that while libertarians were less likely to approve of nudges than those without libertarian dispositions, attitudes about particular policies turned out to be a far more significant predictor than attitudes about libertarianism in general.

Tannenbaum et al. used the same basic strategy to test the responses of actual policymakers, consisting of US city mayors and high-level public servants in state and local governments. They asked the participants to read about two kinds of automatic enrollment defaults. Half read a scenario in which low-income earners were automatically defaulted to receive supplemental food assistance benefits, and half read a scenario in which high-income earners were automatically defaulted to receive capital gains tax benefits. Policymakers were explicitly reminded that the task was the evaluation of nudges as general-purpose policy tools. The usual pattern held: The overall assessments of policymakers were greatly affected by the political valence of the examples.

In sum, "people find nudges more ethically problematic when they are applied to policy objectives they oppose, or when applied by policymakers they oppose, while they find the same nudges more acceptable when they are applied to political objectives they support or by policymakers they support."[11] It would not of course be surprising to find that people favor nudges that support their own goals and reject nudges that undermine those goals. What is more interesting is that many people seem not to have strong or firm judgments about nudges, taken simply as such. Particular examples drive their general views—perhaps because the examples create some kind of affective reaction to the broad category, perhaps because the examples are taken to convey information about how nudges would actually be used (which should of course bear on the overall evaluation). In this respect, people use the examples as heuristics, or mental shortcuts, in answering the broader and more difficult question.

11 *Id.* at 1.

There is a clear implication here for the political economy of nudging: Citizens' judgments about the ethics of nudging, and even the general enterprise, are likely to be, in significant part, an artifact of their substantive judgments about the specific directions in which they think people are likely to be nudged. It is noteworthy that in the United Kingdom, nudging has been prominently associated with the Conservative Party (and Prime Minister David Cameron), which has likely reduced concern from the right (and perhaps heightened concern from the left). This point should not be taken too far. As we have seen, even those who strongly support an incumbent president would be likely to object strenuously if he imposed a nudge that entrenched himself (as, for example, through a system of default voting). In egregious cases of self-dealing, or of violations of widely held social norms, citizens of a free society (or even an unfree one) might well be outraged whatever they think of the underlying substance. But within certain limits, political assessments are likely to reflect political judgments.

We conclude with two general points. First, most Americans are supportive of nudges of the kind that democratic societies have adopted or seriously considered in the recent past. Second, that support diminishes when people distrust the motivations of the choice architects, or when they fear that because of inertia and inattention, citizens might end up with outcomes that are inconsistent with their values or their interests. In particular, Americans object to situations in which choice architects produce outcomes by which people lose money, or other things of importance, without their explicit consent.

4

EUROPE

In many ways, the United States has a distinctive culture. Both scholars and politicians have explored the idea of "American exceptionalism."[1] According to a conventional account, Americans have a strong conception of freedom—perhaps a result of the absence of any kind of feudal past—which leads them to unusually high levels of distrust of government. With respect to nudging, we have not found high levels of distrust of government. But it might well be expected that European nations, with their different cultures and traditions, would show markedly different kinds of reactions and perhaps greater receptivity.

We report here the results of surveys in six nations in Europe: Denmark, France, Germany, Hungary, Italy, and the United Kingdom.[2] Our choice of those nations was of course selective; many European nations are missing (and we will introduce more in later chapters). But there was a method to our

---

1 See, e.g., Seymour Martin Lipset, *American Exceptionalism* (1997).
2 An earlier version of this chapter has been published as: Lucia A. Reisch and Cass R. Sunstein (2016), Do Europeans Like Nudges? JJDM 11(4), 310–25. See also Caezilia Loibl, Cass R. Sunstein, Julius Rauber and Lucia A. Reisch (2018), Which Europeans like nudges? Approval and Controversy in Four European Countries. *Journal of Consumer Affairs*, 52(3), 655–688 (for a deeper analysis of the same data set).

madness. We sought to represent different cultural and geographic regions of Europe as well as different socio-economic regimes and political traditions:

- a Nordic welfare state, which might be thought to be especially receptive to nudging (Denmark);
- a social market economy often thought to have a deep, historically grounded distrust of paternalism, growing out of the Cold War and Stasi experience (Germany);
- a Central European post-socialist country (Hungary);
- two Southern European countries with different political regimes, problems, strengths, and experiences (France and Italy); and
- the United Kingdom, which has helped to spearhead nudging as a policy tool worldwide since 2010, and hence had several years of debate on that topic.

Our major findings are simple and (we think) surprising. As in the United States, so too in the nations explored here: If people believe that a nudge has legitimate goals, and think that it fits with the interests or values of most people, they are overwhelmingly likely to favor it. With only modest qualifications, there is broad support, throughout the six nations, for 12 of the 15 nudges that we tested—and broad opposition, throughout those nations, to the remaining three nudges. In that respect, we find a substantial consensus among disparate nations. (The Bill of Rights for Nudging, discussed in Chapter 9, is meant to apply in all nations.)

Two of the three rejected nudges run afoul of a principle, noted in Chapter 1, on which there is apparently a European consensus: The government should not take people's money without their affirmative consent, even for a good cause. With respect to both charitable donations and carbon offsets, majorities believe default rules to be unacceptable because they offend that principle. We suspect that this finding reflects a broadly held commitment to the idea that by default, people are entitled to keep their own resources; without a clear statement of their own intentions, those resources should remain theirs. There is an evident connection between this finding and the well-known behavioral phenomenon of loss aversion.

Like Americans, people in the covered European countries also reject a nudge that is unambiguously manipulative: a subliminal advertising campaign in movie theaters, designed to convince people not to smoke and overeat. Subliminal advertising can be seen as a defining example of manipulation, because it appeals to people's unconscious processing.

Notwithstanding the general consensus, we find a noteworthy division among nations. While majorities in both Denmark and Hungary are supportive of many nudges, citizens of those nations show significantly[3] lower levels of receptivity to them than do citizens of France, Germany, Italy, and the United Kingdom. Interestingly, however, we do not find, within European nations, consistent and clear associations between party affiliations and approval or disapproval of nudges.

The study

Sampling and survey

We used nationally representative online surveys in six European nations: Denmark, France, Germany, Hungary, Italy, with about 1,000 respondents each, and the United Kingdom, with about 2,000 respondents. Because the respective nation's online population nearly equals the full population in all six countries, and because a stratified sample was used, we can assume almost full representativeness of the surveys. At the same time, we are aware of the limitation that online representativeness does not fully equal ad hoc representativeness.

The survey questionnaire built on that used in Chapter 1. To adjust to the European setting (some of the US nudges are already imposed in Europe) and also to be able to attain a representative sample in six countries, the number of items was reduced to 15. We picked 13 from the US survey and added two additional interventions that had been recently discussed in European politics: (1) requiring supermarket chains to keep cashiers free of sweets (Nudge 14) and (2) requiring canteens in public institutions to have one meat-free day per week (Nudge 15, which, admittedly, is not quite a nudge because it does not preserve freedom of choice; we call it Nudge 15 only for purposes of exposition). The selection covered a wide range of types of nudges: educative nudges, such as information campaigns, and defaults (i.e., different levels of intrusion); noneducative nudges targeting automatic System 1 and educative nudges targeting deliberative System 2 (Chapter 7 focuses on these); nudges covering different areas such as health/food, energy/climate, sustainability, organ donation, and online contracts (see Table 4.1).

We emphasize that as in the US survey, these interventions were deliberately skeletal—for example, we did not identify them with any particular

---

3 We conducted chi-square tests showing significant differences between the two groups of countries for 14 out of 15 nudges.

Table 4.1 The 15 items of the survey

---

1. The federal government requires calorie labels at chain restaurants (such as McDonald's and Burger King).
2. The federal government requires a "traffic lights" system for food, by which healthy foods would be sold with a small green label, unhealthy foods with a small red label, and foods that are neither especially healthy nor especially unhealthy with a small yellow label.
3. The federal government encourages (without requiring) electricity providers to adopt a system in which consumers would be automatically enrolled in a "green" (environmentally friendly) energy supplier, but could opt out if they wished.
4. A state law requiring people to say, when they obtain their driver's license, whether they want to be organ donors.
5. A state law requires all large grocery stores to place their most healthy foods in a prominent, visible location.
6. To reduce deaths and injuries associated with distracted driving, the national government adopts a public education campaign, consisting of vivid and sometimes graphic stories and images, designed to discourage people from texting, emailing, or talking on their cellphones while driving.
7. To reduce childhood obesity, the national government adopts a public education campaign, consisting of information that parents can use to make healthier choices for their children.
8. The federal government requires movie theaters to provide subliminal advertisements (i.e., advertisements that go by so quickly that people are not consciously aware of them) designed to discourage people from smoking and overeating.
9. The federal government requires airlines to charge people, with their airline tickets, a specific amount to offset their carbon emissions (about 10 Euro per ticket); under the program, people can opt out of the payment if they explicitly say that they do not want to pay it.
10. The federal government requires labels on products that have unusually high levels of salt, as in, "This product has been found to contain unusually high levels of salt, which may be harmful to your health."
11. The federal government assumes, on tax returns, that people want to donate 50 Euro to the Red Cross (or to another good cause), subject to opt out if people explicitly say that they do not want to make that donation.
12. The federal government requires movie theaters to run public education messages designed to discourage people from smoking and overeating.

13. The federal government requires large electricity providers to adopt a system in which consumers would be automatically enrolled with a "green" (environmentally friendly) energy supplier, but could opt out if they wished.
14. To halt the rising obesity problem, the federal government requires large supermarket chains to keep cashier areas free of sweets.
15. For reasons of public health and climate protection, the federal government requires canteens in public institutions (schools, public administrations, and similar) to have one meat-free day per week.

---

source (e.g., a leader or a party), and we did not specify the process from which the nudges emerged (e.g., with or without public support). While it would be valuable to test whether and to what extent such characteristics affect people's judgments, our goal here was to examine those judgments without any knowledge of them.

The questionnaire was fully structured and questions were randomized. Respondents were required to follow the questions in the given order and wording. Each item was shown on a single screen. Respondents were asked: "Do you approve or disapprove of the following hypothetical policy?" The two possible answers were displayed in a column ("approve" first, "disapprove" second). The English version was taken as a reference point for the translations and re-translations into the respective languages. In the Danish and Hungarian questionnaire as well as the one for the UK, the currencies were adapted: Euros were replaced by the equivalent amount in Danish kroners, Hungarian forints and British pounds respectively. Details of both sampling and survey can be found in the appendix of this chapter.

The surveys were copy-tested and run by the ISO-certified market research organization GFK (Gesellschaft für Konsumforschung) during the first two weeks in September 2015. This was just before European countries were struck by the so-called "refugee crisis" that has had (and still has to date) an immense impact on the public's views on politics and government policies in Europe, shifting political attitudes markedly to populistic parties on the political right.

The fifteen interventions

An overview of the assessment of all nudges in all countries is provided in Table 4.2. With some exceptions (notably, subliminal advertising which

Table 4.2 Overview on approval rates for the 15 nudges in the six surveyed countries

		IT	UK	FR	DE	HU	DK
1	Requiring calorie labels in chain restaurants	86	85	85	84	74	63
2	Requiring traffic-light labels signaling healthiness of food	77	86	74	79	62	52
3	Encouraging defaulting customers into green energy providers	76	65	61	69	72	63
4	Law requiring active choice regarding organ donation on obtaining the driver's license	72	71	62	49	54	62
5	Law requiring supportive choice architecture for healthy food in large grocery stores	78	74	85	63	59	48
6	Public education campaign with vivid pictures against distracted driving	87	88	86	82	76	81
7	Public education campaign for parents promoting healthier food for their children to fight childhood obesity	89	88	89	90	82	82
8	Requiring subliminal advertising in movie theatres against smoking and overeating	54	49	40	42	37	25
9	Requiring airlines to charge their customers a carbon emission compensation fee	40	46	34	43	18	35
10	Requiring industry to put warning labels on food with high salt content	83	88	90	73	69	69
11	Default citizens to donate 50 Euro for the Red Cross on a tax return	48	25	29	23	37	14
12	Requiring movie theatres to run information campaigns against smoking and overeating	77	67	66	63	40	35
13	Requiring energy providers to default customers into green energy	74	65	57	67	65	55
14	Requiring sweet-free cashier zones in supermarkets	54	82	75	69	44	57
15	Requiring one meat-free day in public canteens	72	52	62	55	46	30

Note: Total support in percentages; unweighted results.

does not qualify as a "nudge," mandated greenhouse gas compensation in air travel, default donation on a tax return, and, to a lesser degree, mandated information campaigns against smoking and overeating as well as meat-free days), we find majority approval in all countries.

For further analyses and exposition here, we categorize the interventions in terms of increasing intrusiveness, resulting in five groups, calculated as mean approval in percentages:

1) *purely government campaigns* to educate people about childhood obesity, distracted driving, and smoking and overeating;
2) *mandatory information nudges*, imposed by government on the private sector, requiring disclosure of nutritional value and health risks of food (calorie labels, high levels of salt, nutritional traffic lights);
3) *mandatory default rules*, imposed by government on the private sector, involving green energy provision, carbon emissions charges, and donations to the Red Cross, along with mandatory choice architecture for retailers to support healthy foods, and mandatory active choice on organ donation;
4) *mandatory subliminal advertising*, imposed by government on movie theaters, to discourage people from smoking and overeating;
5) *mandatory choice architecture* involving supermarkets, a nudge for consumers (sweet-free cashier zones) and also choice editing that goes beyond mere nudging (meat-free days in public cafeterias).

Socio-demographic variables and political preference

A number of socio-demographic variables were collected in the six countries. Due to the limited comparability across countries of most of those variables, we report on only two that are robust: age and gender.

We also report on political preference, measured by asking for whom the respondent voted in the last national elections ("When you think about the last national election, which party did you vote for?"). On the basis of parliamentary groups represented in the European Parliament as well as expert advice, we grouped the political parties into six clusters: conservative/ Christian democratic; left wing/socialist/communist; liberal; green; populist; and "other." While it was obvious that this instrument is rather rough and quite difficult to apply for some countries and parties, we assumed that if they exist, distinct partisan differences would be traceable. Details can be found in Tables A4.2 and A4.3 in the appendix of this chapter.

Statistical analysis

In a first step, we focused on the main results of the analysis of the frequencies regarding approval/disapproval for individual nudges by country. Approval rates are presented in Figures 4.1–4.5. In a next step, we checked for significant differences in approval rates depending on socio-demographic variables and political preferences within countries. As the data has a nested structure, we ran a multilevel regression analysis with the specification of a two-level random intercept model where the first level is country and the second is the individual respondent. In samples such as ours, individual observations are generally not independent, as individuals within one country tend to be more similar to each other than across countries.

We estimated the multilevel regression for each level of intrusion (from weak to excessive), with the approval rates being the dependent variables. For this, we calculated the mean approval in percentages by the level of intrusiveness. As outlined above, we categorize the 15 nudges in terms of increasing intrusiveness, resulting in five groups. As independent variables we use age, gender, and political attitude on the individual level, and country on the country level.

Results

Information: Government campaigns

We tested three nudges that seem minimally intrusive, in the sense that they involve the mere provision of information by the government. The nudges involved (1) public education campaigns to reduce childhood obesity, (2) similar campaigns to reduce deaths and injuries from distracted driving, and (3) similar campaigns, in movie theaters, to discourage people from smoking and overeating.

Over all countries, the average approval rate for all three nudges is 76.9 percent. In all six nations, both (1) and (2) received overwhelming support (see Figure 4.1). We expected (3) to be more controversial, and it was. It did receive majority support in Italy, the United Kingdom, France, and Germany, but the levels were lower than for (1) and (2), and in Denmark and Hungary, majorities disapproved (significant difference between the two groups of countries confirmed).

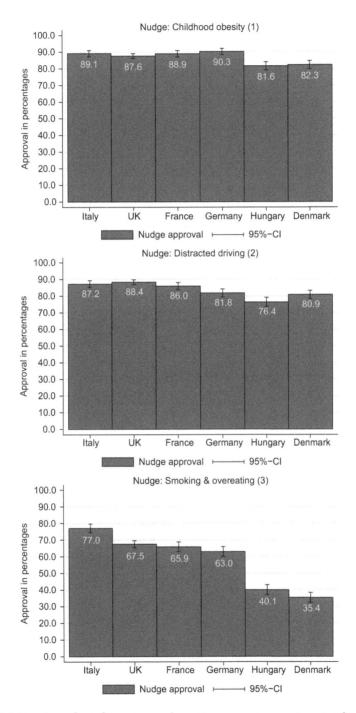

Figure 4.1 Bar charts for information nudges: Government campaigns, total support in % (unweighted)

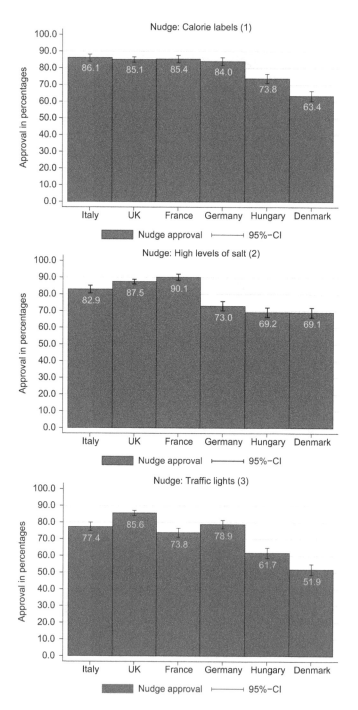

Figure 4.2 Bar charts for information nudges, governmentally mandated, total support in % (unweighted)

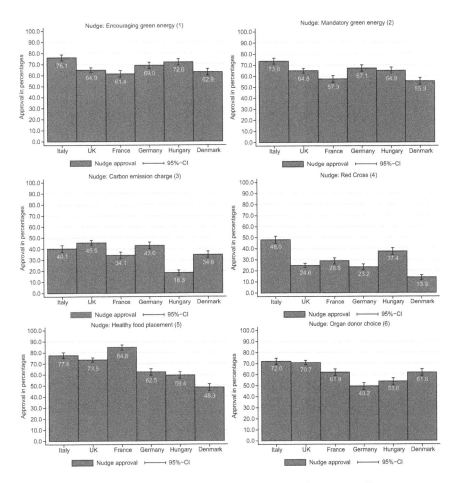

Figure 4.3 Bar charts for default rules, total support in % (unweighted)

Information: Governmentally mandated nudges

We tested three informational nudges that took the form of mandates on the private sector, designed to promote healthy eating: (1) calorie labels, (2) salt labels (for products with particularly high levels), and (3) a "traffic lights" system for more or less healthy food. Because such nudges require action by private institutions (companies), they might seem more intrusive than educational campaigns by the government itself. But all three obtained majority support, with an average approval of 78.0 percent across all six nations (see Figure 4.2). The most noteworthy division here is again between Denmark and Hungary on the

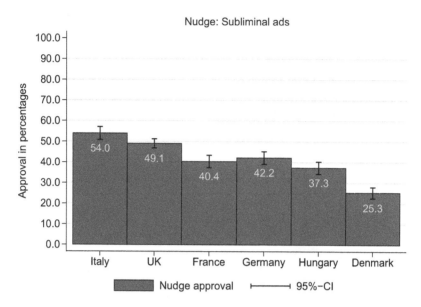

Figure 4.4 Bar chart for subliminal ads, total support in % (unweighted)

one hand and Italy, the United Kingdom, France, and Germany on the other. The first two showed significantly lower levels of support, though majorities approved.

Default rules

Default rules are often the most prominent and effective nudges. We asked respondents about five potentially controversial kinds: (1) government encouragement (without a mandate) of automatic enrollment in green energy; (2) governmentally mandated green energy defaults; (3) defaulting air travelers into the payment of carbon offsets; (4) defaulting taxpayers into a 50 Euro (or equivalent) payment to the Red Cross; (5) requiring large grocery stores to place healthy foods in a prominent, accessible location. We also asked respondents about (6) requiring people to say, when they receive a driver's license, whether they wanted to be organ donors. Active choosing is not a default rule, but because it is a form of choice architecture designed to elicit people's preferences, we group it with default rules here.

On average, 54.8 percent approved default rules across the six countries. In all nations, (1) and (2) received strong majority support (see Figure 4.3). Majorities in all nations except Denmark favored (5).

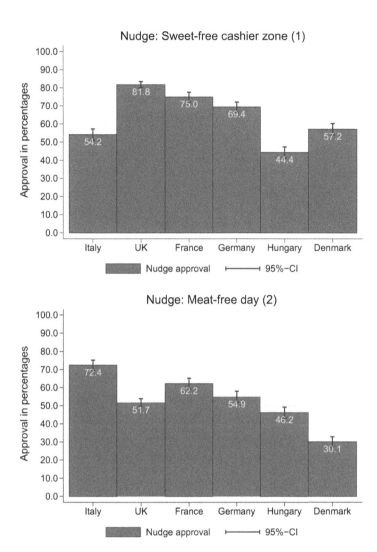

Figure 4.5 Bar charts for other mandates

In all nations, both (3) and (4) were rejected by substantial majorities (see Figure 4.3), which helps account for the relatively small margin of majority support for all interventions in this category. Interestingly, the nudge "encouragement of green energy" (1) is the only one without a significant difference between the two groups of countries. There was majority approval of (6) in all countries, with the interesting exception of Germany.

Manipulation: Subliminal advertising

Finally, we asked respondents about an intervention that might be expected to be widely rejected as a defining example of manipulation: compulsory subliminal advertising in movie theaters, designed to discourage smoking and overeating. And indeed, it was rejected, but not exactly widely, with an average approval rate of 42.5 percent, and with the puzzling qualification that in Italy and the United Kingdom we find majority or near-majority support (see Figure 4.4).

Other mandates

Requiring (1) sweet-free cashier areas and (2) meat-free days in cafeterias in public institutions are relatively strong government interventions. Both ideas have produced controversy in European politics. To our knowledge, while retailers and canteens in some countries increasingly experiment with such choice architecture, they have not been tested in representative European surveys before. Sweet-free cashier areas can be regarded as a nudge for consumers; meat-free days go far beyond a nudge.

The average approval rate across countries is 59.6 percent. Results in Figure 4.5 show approval for sweet-free cashier zones in supermarkets by majorities in all countries, except for Hungary. Somewhat surprisingly, even a meat-free day in cafeterias in public institutions is approved by majorities, except for Hungary and Denmark.

Approval rates: Sex, age, and politics

We found broad support for most of the 15 nudges that we tested, notwithstanding some striking differences across the six countries (as shown in Figures 4.1–4.5). At the same time, we explored whether there might be differences in approval across demographic categories and among groups with different political preferences within countries or groups of countries. We ran a multilevel regression analysis which provided clear results (presented in Table A4.4 in the appendix).

The basic picture is that except for gender (females are slightly more positive), socio-economic characteristics do not significantly influence people's attitude towards the nudges in the six countries. We do see a tendency for older respondents to be more in favor of information nudges and defaults, but the effect is not a strong one and not the same in all six countries. Yet again, our results suggest that it is the aim that the government wants to achieve with the nudge that determines approval. But as the different results in Denmark and Hungary show, country differences can matter a great deal.

The overall pattern

The best explanation for the overall pattern of results is straightforward. As in the United States, so too in Europe: When Europeans believe that a nudge has legitimate purposes and is consistent with the interests or values of most people, majorities are likely to support it. At least if nudges are presented in the simple form used here, there is no opposition to nudging as such, even if it takes the form of default rules or other arguably aggressive forms of choice architecture.

It would not be unreasonable to speculate that people might have some kind of informal hierarchy in mind, corresponding to their intuitions about intrusiveness—with, perhaps, government educational campaigns being the weakest kind of nudge, and default rules the strongest, while mandatory information disclosure from the private sector might be found in the middle. But our results suggest that any informal hierarchy—even if it exists—is not the principal driver of people's judgments. What most matters is what the nudge is trying to achieve. Most of the nudges we tested were designed to promote health, safety, and clean energy, and people generally approve of them, because they endorse those goals.

Importantly, our survey did not provide people with information about benefits and costs, and their responses probably reflect intuitive (and potentially inaccurate) judgments about likely consequences. Suppose, for example, that people were informed that a certain educational campaign was expensive to implement and would have little or no effect. If so, people would be unlikely to support it. That is of course an extreme case. It would be interesting to test whether the high levels of support would increase with favorable benefit-cost ratios and if they would fall with less favorable ones. In Chapter 7, we shall offer some evidence on that question. Our claim about high levels of European support for nudging depends, of course, on how Europeans respond without being given relevant information. In our view, it is relevant and important to find high levels of receptivity to identifiable policy initiatives in the abstract, not least because people's judgments will inevitably be affected by their own priors about effectiveness.

One of our most noteworthy findings is that most Europeans, like most Americans, reject nudges that take people's money without their affirmative consent, even if the underlying cause is appealing. Apparently they do not want choice architects to produce economic or other losses by using people's inertia or inattention against them. There appears to be a general moral principle here, one that imposes a presumptive barrier to certain nudges: *If people are to give up some part of their existing holdings, it must be because they have affirmatively indicated their willingness to do so.* We have evidence that this is a widely shared moral principle. It might anchor a range of ethical judgments and may even lie at the root of contract law, which often calls for explicit consent before certain losses can occur.

At the same time, this principle leaves many open questions; it is also subject to qualifications. Our own findings suggest that it applies to money (and also bodily parts). Would it apply to any form of property (for example, real property or copyright)? We suspect so. Would it also apply to time? Again we suspect so. Recall that if the government is taking money from people's current selves for the benefit of their future selves, Americans do not object (see Chapter 2); the same point holds for citizens of several European nations as well. And if the point of the default rule is to compensate victims of wrongdoing, the principle is unlikely to be violated at all; people would not complain if thieves were required to return stolen money. As we have noted, the principle is not meant as a general attack on the tax system.

But our evidence suggests that in any stylized case in which the government is presuming something like a donation—as when a default rule requires such a donation without explicit consent—most people will react unfavorably. Perhaps they believe that donations, as such, require personal responsibility. Far more work remains to be done on these questions, above all to identify the boundary conditions of what we have described as a general moral principle.

In philosophical circles, there is an extensive literature on the subject of manipulation. In ordinary language, the term is one of opprobrium, which raises two distinct questions: What, exactly, is manipulation, and what is wrong with it? We do not yet have anything like a "map" to people's answers to those questions. But subliminal advertising can be taken as a defining example of unacceptable manipulation, because it influences people without engaging their conscious or deliberative capacities. The influence occurs surreptitiously. If the government engages in subliminal advertising, people will not approve, because the use of such advertising seems unambiguously manipulative.

National characteristics

Of the six nations, Italy and the UK are most favorably disposed toward the nudges that we tested. In Italy, only one nudge (Nudge 14: sweet-free cashier zones in supermarkets) is less popular than in most of the other countries. Similarly, the UK is in the top ranks of approval 11 out of 15 times. (France and Germany cannot be so clearly ranked.) It is reasonable to ask why Italy and the UK are comparatively receptive. We do not have an answer to that question, but it is worthwhile to note that Italy is not known to have a tradition or recent history of antipathy to paternalistic interventions, and perhaps the recent experience of the UK, involving many uses of behavioral science, has influenced public opinion.[4]

Both Hungary and Denmark are consistently less favorably disposed toward nudges in general. The case of Hungary is not so puzzling. In that nation, there is widespread distrust of social institutions, which has been below the Organisation for Economic Co-operation and Development (OECD) average for a long time.[5] The legacy of Communism may lead Hungarians to disapprove of government in general. At the same time, Hungary is the country (from our subset) with the highest corruption index, sliding even deeper down in past years.[6] Moreover, it is below the OECD level in voting in national elections.[7] It is safe to hypothesize that this lack of confidence did not improve with the Orban government. The Hungarian findings also cast light on differences, within nations, with respect to nudges: Citizens who distrust their government, or government in general, will be less likely to approve of nudges, even if they approve of the particular ends that those nudges would promote.[8] We shall explore this issue in detail in Chapter 6.

---

4 See David Halpern, *Inside the Nudge Unit: How Small Changes Can Make a Big Difference* (2015).

5 See Organisation for Economic Co-operation and Development, *Confidence in Social Institutions. Society at a Glance 2011: OECD Social Indicators* (2011). The OECD Confidence in National Institutions Index is based on the Gallup World Poll; it is based on questions regarding confidence in the military, the judiciary and the national government. See also the Transparency International Corruption Index at www.transparency.org/country/HUN.

6 See *Id.*

7 See Organisation for Economic Co-operation and Development (OECD) (2011), Voting. In *Society at a Glance 2011: OECD Social Indicators.* http://dx.doi.org/10.1787/soc_glance-2011-29-en. However, voting in the UK and France is even lower.

8 For a related finding, *see* David Tannenbaum et al., On the Misplaced Politics of Behavioural Policy Interventions, *Nature Human Behaviour* 1(0130) (2017).

With respect to Denmark, our findings are far more difficult to explain. That nation is not exactly known for its distrust of government, or for its firm opposition to anything that smacks of paternalism. Denmark has had one of the highest levels of trust in government from all OECD countries.[9] However, while trust in politicians on a communal and regional level has remained high, there has been a decline in trust in national politicians and government over the last years. The results of a national survey in 2015 show that the trust in Danish politicians fell from 70 percent in 2007 to 28 percent in June 2015, an all-time low.[10] In particular, our results might be related to distrust in the new conservative policy landscape after the federal elections in 2015. The new government had just started its term a few months before the survey was executed. But overall, Denmark regularly ranks first or second in international corruption rankings and trust in government is still comparatively high. Some controversial health-related interventions in Denmark (including a tax on foods with high levels of saturated fats) might have contributed to our findings.

Politics and demographics

We do not find clear differences across party lines within Europe. One of our main findings, and among the most surprising, is that party affiliations are not correlated in any systematic way with support for the nudges we tested. Within countries, however, there are some weak correlations and two overall patterns. (1) In France, Green Party and left-wing supporters are more favorably disposed toward the tested nudges. (2) In the United Kingdom, people who have voted for populist parties are particularly skeptical toward information nudges. (3) Over all countries, European liberals are somewhat less inclined to favor health nudges. (4) Over all countries, Green Party voters are somewhat more inclined to favor environmental nudges (not surprisingly). We suggest, however, that these findings should be taken with some caution, in light of our rough measurement of political preferences (most recent vote) and the clustering of political parties in Europe.

9   *See* EU European Commission, *Public Opinion in the European Union.* Standard Eurobarometer No. 83. Brussels: EC (2014). *See also* Organisation for Economic Co-operation and Development, Confidence in Social Institutions. In *Society at a Glance 2011:OECD Social Indicators* (2011).

10   www.altinget.dk/artikel/historisk-faa-danskere-stoler-paa-politikerne?ref=newslett er&refid=17813&SNSubscribed=true&utm_source=Nyhedsbrev&utm_medium=e-mail&utm_campaign=altingetdk.

With respect to demographic differences, only one characteristic seems to be correlated with people's attitudes toward the nudges we tested: gender. Women favor such nudges more than men do, with a less pronounced (but still significant) gender divide in France and Denmark. In general, we did not otherwise find statistically significant differences. With respect to other demographic characteristics, we identified no relevant correlations.

Larger themes

In Europe, there is strong majority support for nudges of the sort that have been adopted, or under serious consideration, in democratic nations. If respondents believe that a nudge has legitimate goals, and that it fits with the interests or values of most people, they are likely to favor it. At the same time, the citizens of six nations reject nudges that offend two principles that command a consensus: First, government should not take people's money without their explicit consent; and second, government should not manipulate people (at least in the defining case of subliminal advertising).

Despite the general European consensus, we find markedly lower levels of support for nudges in two nations: Hungary and Denmark. In Hungary, this finding is best explained by reference to reduced levels of trust for government—a point that confirms the intuition that when distrust of the competence or the motivation of public officials is high, even choice-preserving interventions will be unwelcome. Lower levels of support in Denmark are more challenging to explain.

In Europe, we have generally been unable to link political affiliations or demographic variables to support for (or opposition to) nudges. Among the few exceptions are: somewhat stronger female approval for the tested nudges; a tendency (as expected) for Green Party voters to support environmental nudges; and lower levels of support among European liberals for health nudges.

We do not doubt that people with certain political convictions are a bit like the citizens of Hungary and Denmark, and therefore suspicious of any government action, whether it consists of nudges, taxes, subsidies, or mandates. But notably, we have been unable to find clear and consistent evidence to this effect for any political party within Europe. It is also true that some nudges seem to split Europeans along political lines. But when this is so, it is because of the particular direction in which people are being nudged—not because they are being nudged as such.

Appendix to Chapter 4

Table A4.1 Samples, sampling, and methodology

Country	Sample size	Representativeness	Survey method	Weighting method	Sample	Recruiting for the panel	Census/Population	Frame of the survey
Italy	N=1,011	Online representative for gender, age, region	CAWI Omnibus	No weighting	Quota sampling	Offline and online	35 mio internet users, 18–64 years	No frames
UK	N=2,033	F2f representative for gender, age, region	CAWI Omnibus	RIM	Quota sampling	Online	50.9 mio internet users, 18+ years	About saving and spending habits
France	N=1,022	F2f representative for gender, age, region	CAWI Omnibus	Target	Quota sampling	Online	41.05 mio internet users, 16–64 years	About views on the Ukraine
Germany	N=1,012	Online representative for gender, age, region	CAWI Omnibus	RIM	Quota sampling	Offline and online	55.06 mio internet users, 14+ years	About views on the economy
Hungary	N=1,001	F2f representative for gender, age, region	CAWI ad hoc	RIM	Quota sampling	Offline	7.35 mio internet users, 15–69 years	Ad hoc, no other frames
Denmark	N=1,000	F2f representative for gender, age, region	CAWI Omnibus	Target	Quota sampling	Offline	4.54 mio internet users, 18+ years	About consumer goods and the Great Belt Bridge

Notes: "f2f (face to face) representative" means representative for the resident population. "Online representative" means representative for private internet users. "CAWI" means Computer Assisted Web Interview. "Ad hoc" is used in Hungary where no omnibus survey was available. "RIM (Random Iterative Method) weighting" and "target weighting" are statistical weighting methods applied to ensure validity of the multidimensional model when not every group of the population is equally represented in a sample. "Quota sampling" means that data collection was done following quotas for specific socio-demographic characteristics, and then the observations were weighted according to their frequency in the population. (The exception is Italy, where no weighting was needed.) "Frames" might unintendedly influence answers in omnibus surveys with multiple unrelated questionnaires. While frames cannot be avoided in practice, it is important to know which questions had been asked before the question of interest to estimate unintended influence. "Mio" means million.

Table A4.2 Overview of political parties in the surveyed countries

Italy	UK	France	Germany	Hungary	Denmark
Partito Democratico (PD)	Conservative	Socialiste, républicain et citoyen	CDU/CSU	Fidesz—KDNP	Socialdemokra-terne (A)
Movimento 5 Stelle	Labour	Les Républicains	SPD	Jobbik	Dansk Folkeparti (O)
Il Popolo della Libertà (PdL)	SNP (Scotland)	Union des démocrates et indépendants	Grüne	MSZP	Venstre (V)
Scelta Civica con Monti per l'Italia	Liberal Democrats	Radical, républicain, démocrate et progressiste	Die Linke	Demokratikus Koalíció (DK)	Enhedslisten (Ø)
Sinistra Ecologia Libertà (SEL)	Plaid Cymru (Wales)	Écologiste	FDP	Lehet Más a Politika (LMP)	Liberal Alliance (I)
Lega Nord	UK Independence Party	Gauche démocrate et républicaine	Piraten	Együtt 2014	Alternativet (Å)
Fratelli d'Italia	Green Party	Front National	AfD	Párbeszéd Magyarországért (PM)	Det Radikale Venstre (B)
Unione di Centro			Freie Wähler		Socialistisk Folkeparti (F)
Others	Others	Others	Others	Others	Others
I didn't vote.	I didn't vote.	I didn't vote.	I didn't vote.	I didn't vote.	I didn't vote.
Don't know / no answer	Don't know / no answer	Don't know / no answer	Don't know / no answer	Don't know / no answer	Don't know / no answer

Table A4.3 Clusters of the political parties in the surveyed countries

Country	Political attitude cluster				
	Conservative	Left-wing	Liberal	Green	Populists & others
Italy	Il Popolo delle Libertà (PdL) Unione di Centro	Partito Democratico (PD)	Scelta Civica con Monti per l'Italia	Sinistra Ecologia Libertà (SEL)	Movimento 5 Stelle Lega Nord Fratelli d'Italia Others
United Kingdom	Conservative	Labour	Liberal Democrats	Green	SNP (Scotland) Plaid Cymru (Wales) UK Independence Others
France	Les Républicains Union des démocrates et indépendants	Socialiste, républicain et citoyen Radical, républicain, démocrate et progressiste Gauche démocrate et républicaine		Écologiste	La Front National Others
Germany	Christian Democrats (CDU/CSU)	Sozialdemokraten (SPD) Die Linke	Freie Demokraten (FDP)	Die Grünen	Piraten AfD Freie Wähler Others
Hungary	Fidesz—KDNP	MSZP Demokratikus Koalíció (DK) Együtt 2014		Lehet Más a Politika (LMP) Párbeszéd Magyarországért (PM)	Jobbik Others
Denmark		Socialdemokraterne Enhedslisten Socialistisk Folkeparti	Venstre Liberal Alliance Det Radikale Venstre (social-liberal)	Alternativet	Dansk Folkeparti Others

Note: Reflects the political spectrum in 2015 for national elections.

Table A4.4 Estimates of demographics and political attitude on nudge approval: Multilevel analysis

	(1) Information: Government campaigns	(2) Information: Governmentally mandated nudges	(3) Default rules	(4) Manipulation	(5) Other mandates
Male	-2.105**	-3.160***	-4.509***	-5.217***	-7.661***
	(.671)	(.723)	(.661)	(1.166)	(.879)
	[-3.420,-.790]	[-4.577,-1.742]	[-5.805,-3.213]	[-7.502,-2.932]	[-9.383,-5.939]
Age (categories)	.407***	.127	.705***	.566**	.037
	(.111)	(.120)	(.109)	(.193)	(.146)
	[.189,.625]	[-.108,.362]	[-.920,-.491]	[-.944,-.187]	[-.249,.322]
Political attitude					
Conservative	ref.	ref.	ref.	ref.	ref.
Left-wing	-1.724	-.593	1.153	-7.165***	1.46
	(.987)	(1.064)	(.973)	(1.715)	(1.293)
	[-3.658,.210]	[-2.678,1.492]	[-0.754,3.059]	[-10.526,-3.804]	[-1.074,3.993]
Liberal	-2.88	-7.912***	-3.750*	-13.760***	-6.314**
	(1.618)	(1.745)	(1.595)	(2.809)	(2.120)
	[-6.052,.292]	[-11.332,-4.492]	[-6.876,-.625]	[-19.266,-8.255]	[-10.468,-2.159]
Green	-.920	-1.774	5.131***	-19.736***	6.168**
	(1.526)	(1.645)	(1.504)	(2.651)	(1.999)
	[-3.910,2.071]	[-4.999,1.450]	[2.183,8.079]	[-24.931,-14.540]	[2.250,10.085]
Populist & others	-5.370***	-5.679***	-3.170**	-7.436***	-4.804**
	(1.128)	(1.217)	(1.112)	(1.960)	(1.478)
	[-7.582,-3.159]	[-8.064,-3.295]	[-5.350,-0.990]	[-11.277,-3.595]	[-7.701,-1.907]

(Continued)

	(1) Information: Government campaigns	(2) Information: Governmentally mandated nudges	(3) Default rules	(4) Manipulation	(5) Other mandates
Don't know / did not vote	−5.749***	−6.554***	−2.724**	−8.024***	−4.197**
	(1.027)	(1.108)	(1.012)	(1.784)	(1.346)
	[−7.763,−3.736]	[−8.724,−4.383]	[−4.708,−0.739]	[−11.521,−4.528]	[−6.834,−1.560]
Obs.	7,079	7,079	7,079	7,079	7,079
Wald Chi^2	69.34	84.81	141.19	89.23	132.63
p-value	(.000)	(.000)	(.000)	(.000)	(.000)
ICC (country)	.069	.076	.043	.027	.070
	(.037)	(.041)	(.024)	(.016)	(.038)

Note: * $p \leq .05$; ** $p \leq .01$; *** $p \leq .001$. Estimates of a 2-level random intercept model. Standard errors (Confidence intervals) in parentheses. Dependent variables are the average nudge groups by intrusiveness (Min: 0; Max: 100). The intraclass correlation coefficient (ICC) is the proportion of total variance that is attributed to the cluster "country." "Ref." means "reference variable", i.e., a variable that serves as a baseline to measure the deviation of other related variables.

5

A GLOBAL CONSENSUS? NOT QUITE

The discussion can be taken to offer five general lessons. First, citizens in diverse nations generally approve of nudges, at least of the kind that have been adopted or are under serious consideration in recent years. Second, citizens do not approve of nudges that they perceive to be inconsistent with the interests or values of most choosers, such as a default rule by which men's last name would automatically change to that of their wives. Third, citizens do not approve of nudges that are perceived as having an illicit goal, such as religious or political favoritism. Fourth, citizens object to manipulation, but they define it quite narrowly, as in the case of subliminal advertising. Fifth, and quite surprisingly, political affiliation is generally a weak predictor of citizens' reactions to the tested nudges.

In this chapter, we offer results from eight countries: Australia, Brazil, Canada, China, Japan, Russia, South Africa, and South Korea. These nations were chosen in order to obtain a broad sample of countries with diversity along identifiable lines. We include countries widely distributed on a scale from liberal democracies with freedom of speech to authoritarian one-party regimes. We also include four of the five BRICS countries (BRICS is the acronym for an association of five major emerging national economies: Brazil, Russia, India, China, and South Africa).[1] The relevant countries have markedly different levels of GDP and welfare. They include countries representing the "cultural clusters" explored in cultural studies literature.[2] Least interestingly, the countries have sufficient internet penetration rates[3] to conduct meaningful online representative surveys.[4]

We conducted such surveys (representative for age, gender, region, and education), providing data from about 1,000 respondents per country, who were asked whether they approve or disapprove of the 15 nudges described in Chapter 4. Again we asked simply for a statement of approval or disapproval, without measuring the intensity of approval or disapproval on any kind of scale. In order to be able to compare and enlarge the overall data set, we used the same survey instrument and largely the same methodology applied in Chapter 4.

In view of the highly preliminary state of existing research, and the inevitability of surprises, our goal was to learn about national similarities and differences, and we did not begin with firm hypotheses. Tentatively, however, we expected to support two hypotheses:

> Hypothesis 1: The apparent cross-national consensus with respect to nudges, reflected in the five lessons from earlier studies, would be found, with modest variations, in all of the nations in our survey, with the exceptions of China and Russia.
>
> Hypothesis 2: As nondemocratic nations, China and Russia would show overwhelmingly high levels of support for nudges of all kinds, either

1 Unfortunately, we could not cover India with our online survey design due to many different languages, a high sample size needed to capture the different regions and minorities, and a surprisingly low internet penetration rate.
2 See Vipin Gupta et al., Cultural Clusters: Methodology and Findings, *J. World Bus.* 37(1) (2002), 11–5; Robert J. House et al., *Culture, Leadership, and Organization: The GLOBE Study of 62 Societies* (2004); Robert J. House et al., *Strategic Leadership Across Cultures: The GLOBE Study of CEO Leadership Behaviour and Effectiveness in 24 Countries* (2014). The ten "culture clusters" used typically in cultural studies (e.g., in the GLOBE study, House et al., 2014) are South Asia, Anglo, Arab/Middle Eastern, Germanic Europe, Latin Europe, Eastern Europe, Confucian Asia, Latin America, (Sub-Sahara) Africa, and Nordic Europe. Together with European data collected in 2015 (see Chapter 3), we cover all clusters except for two ("Southern Asia" and "Middle Eastern").
3 www.internetlivestats.com/internet-users-by-country/.
4 An earlier version of this chapter has been published as: Cass R. Sunstein, Lucia A. Reisch and Julius Rauber, A Worldwide Consensus on Nudging? Not Quite, But Almost, *Regulation and Governance* 12(1), 3–22, doi:10.1111/rego.12161.

because of a belief that disapproval might be punished (even though we guaranteed anonymity), or because disapproval of government policies would be distinctly rare among citizens who are accustomed to autocratic rule.

As we shall see, the first hypothesis was generally supported, but with an important qualification: The first three lessons, and the fifth, can indeed be found in essentially all of the nations that we studied, but the fourth (forbidding manipulation via subliminal advertising) cannot. As we shall also see, the second hypothesis was supported with respect to China but not with respect to Russia (whose citizens look more like those of the United States and Europe). In addition, we found a number of surprises, above all involving Japan (which showed unusually low approval rates) and South Korea (which showed unusually high approval rates).

The most general lesson is that majority support for nudges cuts across many nations with diverse cultures, political inclinations, and histories. At the same time, our largest finding, which we did not anticipate, is that the nations of the world can be provisionally grouped into three categories. The first, consistent with the first hypothesis and the existing US and European data, reflects all of the five lessons sketched above. Of the nations for which data are available, this is the largest group of the nations tested thus far. Call these *principled pro-nudge nations*.

The second category, consistent with data from Denmark and Hungary, generally shows majority approval but significantly lower approval rates; Japan now joins this category. Call these, *cautiously pro-nudge nations*. The third category, identified for the first time here, consists of nations with massively high approval ratings. China and South Korea are the current examples. (Recall that Russia is not included.) Call these, *overwhelmingly pro-nudge nations*.

We suspect that many and probably most other nations would fall into one of these three categories. We cannot, of course, exclude the possibility that some nations would show an altogether different pattern—with, for example, far lower approval ratings than what we find in Denmark, Hungary, and Japan (*anti-nudge nations*), or with divergent approval rates across various categories of nudges (*selectively pro-nudge nations*).

Our main goal in this chapter is to report on the various national findings, without offering a full account of why nations fall into one of the three categories. By themselves, our findings do not provide any such account, and in view of limits in existing knowledge, any speculations will inevitably have an ad hoc character. Nonetheless, we shall not refrain from offering some such speculations here; we shall turn in Chapter 6 to the question of trust.

The study

Sampling and survey

Sampling and survey were performed with the support of Qualtrics, an ISO-certified international market research company. To ensure the necessary level of rigor, we monitored and commented on each step of the sampling and survey implementation. As with the surveys reported in previous chapters, we intended the eight country samples to be online representatives with respect to age, gender, educational level, and region. To reach this high level of representativeness, several steps were undertaken, including oversampling and RIM weighting. (An overview of the weighted and unweighted samples can be found in Table A5.1 in the appendix to this chapter.)

As before, the core instrument is a simple questionnaire with 15 different interventions. Also as before, respondents were asked to indicate for each item whether they "approve" or "do not approve" of this specific "hypothetical policy." The potentially confusing word "nudge" (or the respective translation) was deliberately not used in the survey; rather, the policy instrument was described as simply and intelligibly as possible. We did not intend to frame the policies in a way that would skew people's answers. The 15 items of the questionnaire can be found in Chapter 4.

The items of our questionnaire were first entered in the Qualtrics web interface in October 2016. Qualtrics checked the items in order to ensure that they were understandable and consistent to an English-speaking audience. The questionnaire was translated from English (the blueprint for all country studies) into the respective languages (Brazilian Portuguese, Canadian French, Mandarin, Japanese, Russian, and Korean) and was back-translated by native speakers and corrected accordingly. This additional step was designed to ensure that people would have the same understanding of the items in the different countries and that infrequently used words or concepts would be fully understood and interpreted in the same way. Monetary amounts used in some items were adapted to the specific countries based on the exchange rate of the currency and its average income. As before, the questions were presented in a randomized order.[5]

To ensure high quality samples, we included a range of validity and robustness checks. Apparently inattentive or careless respondents were excluded by employing a time filter (sorting out respondents who used less than half of the median time needed to answer the survey) as well as by adding two attention filters in the survey.[6] Responses were allowed to enter the final sample only when they met these attention standards and were provided by adults (18 years and older) who lived in the respective country and used its official language. The latter was ensured by a language default using the language of the browser of a participant. In Canada, participants could choose between French and English. Respondents also were forced to answer all questions (i.e., no skipping and "cherry picking"). Only fully completed questionnaires were accepted.

Field work started with a soft launch of ten percent of the data in all countries concurrently in November 2016. Results were checked for consistency, validity, and robustness. Minor adaptations were made for the remaining 90 percent of the sampling. Field time ended after about five weeks in December 2016.

Socio-demographics and political attitudes

We collected information on socio-demographic variables and political attitudes. Comparability of socio-demographic variables among the eight countries was given for gender (male/female), age (years), city size (number of inhabitants), relationship status (married/civil partnership; long-term relationship; single; divorced; widowed; others), and number of children.

Comparability is less clear-cut for region, education, and income. "Region" is country-specific, and so we used the categories provided by national statistics; these data are more relevant for discussion of the results within the respective countries than for comparison of countries.

---

5 The full questionnaire as well as complete information on socio-demographic variables and political attitudes can be found in Sunstein et al., *supra* note 62, 17–22.

6 Attention filter 1 (after Nudge 7): "This is an attention filter. Please click on '3' to go on with the survey". Attention filter 2 (after Nudge 15): "This is an attention filter. Please click 'approve' to go on with the survey"—with the order of the two answer categories being switched.

"Education" was measured in two ways: (1) the usual brackets of the countries' statistics ("highest degree reached"), allowing limited comparability; and (2) "number of years of formal education," which can more easily be compared against the backdrop of the respective country specifics such as average education level. "Income" must be understood in light of the country's income distribution and level to be useful; we therefore developed and applied an algorithm based on the gross household median income in each country.

Political attitude was measured in two ways: first, by choosing "political party voted for in the latest election" (except for China, which has a one-party system) from the full set of available political parties in the respective country that received at least five percent of the votes in the last country-wide election; and second, by a self-assessment political preference item ("Where would you place yourself on this scale?") presented as a Likert scale ranging from (1) denoting "extremely liberal (left)" to (7) denoting "extremely conservative (right)." The second approach was introduced as a robustness check, and it also provided quantitative input in the multilevel analysis described in the following paragraph. Admittedly, both measures are rough, and hence our results should be interpreted cautiously.

Results

Approval rates

The country data sets were merged into one data set. Approval rates were calculated per nudge and per country. Due to its nested character, the data were suited for a multilevel analysis. For the latter, five independent variables were constructed, mirroring the analysis of the European country data. As before, the 15 nudges were clustered with respect to their level of intrusiveness in five clusters; average approval rates for each dependent variable were calculated. Coding and analysis was done with SPSS. Analyses were conducted for unweighted and weighted samples.[7]

---

7 There were only marginal differences between the two approaches. Regarding the approval rates, the largest difference between weighted and unweighted samples exists for the nudge "healthy food placement" in Japan, with five percentage points (weighted sample: 47 percent; unweighted sample: 42 percent). For all other nudges, maximum deviation is three percentage points between the weighted and unweighted samples in all countries. With respect to significant coefficients in the multilevel analysis (Table 5.1),

As noted, we categorized the 15 nudges in five levels of depth of intervention: governmental information campaigns (Nudges 6 and 7) (Figure 5.1); mandatory information disclosure requirements imposed by governments (Nudges 1, 2, 10, and 12) (Figure 5.2)[8]; mandatory default rules imposed by governments (Nudges 3, 4, 5, 9, 11, and 13) (Figure 5.3); mandatory subliminal advertising (Nudge 8) (Figure 5.4); and mandatory choice architecture in supermarkets and public cafeterias (Nudge 14 and Nudge 15) (Figure 5.5).

As noted, our findings are generally consistent with Hypothesis 1. With respect to information campaigns, we observe majority support in all eight nations, and consistent with that hypothesis, the similarities are far more noteworthy than the differences. For nudges tackling childhood obesity and distracted driving, the level of support is overwhelming.

Consistent with Hypothesis 1, mandatory information disclosure also receives very high levels of support, and here too, the similarities dwarf the

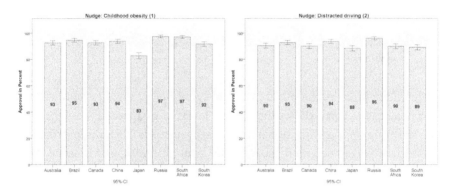

Figure 5.1 General information campaigns. CI, confidence interval

there were only two differences between weighted and unweighted samples: the age coefficient in Column 1 becomes insignificant when using the unweighted sample; the coefficient of "years in school" becomes significant when using the unweighted sample.

8 Note that Nudge 12 ("The federal government requires movie theaters to run public education messages designed to discourage people from smoking and overeating") was, in the present study, moved from Nudge Cluster 1 ("pure governmental information campaigns") to Nudge Cluster 2 ("mandatory disclosure requirements"). This change was a result of what we found to be convincing arguments with respect to our European study (Chapter 3). Statistics show that the results of the European study are still largely—though not fully—comparable with the present one.

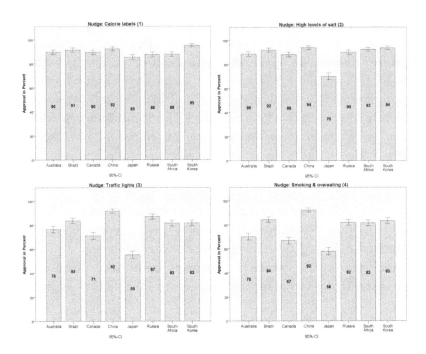

Figure 5.2 Mandatory information imposed by governments. CI, confidence
           interval

differences. Japan is the obvious and only outlier. Majorities do approve,
but in all cases, Japan shows the highest levels of disapproval, in particular
for traffic lights and educational messages against smoking and overeating.

With respect to default rules, approval levels diminish, and in some cases
majorities disapprove. Here again, we find general support for Hypothesis 1.
Consistent with findings in the United States and the previously tested
nations in Europe, strong majorities favor not only encouragement of automatic enrollment in green energy but also a mandate to that effect. (To be
sure, approval rates should be expected to decrease if people were told
that the cost of green energy was higher than that of other sources.) Also
consistent with earlier findings, majorities disapprove of a default carbon
charge and also a default charitable donation. Again, the basic principle
here seems to have something to do with loss aversion: In general, people
do not favor default rules that would take people's money without their
explicit consent.

Because of their high approval rates, China, South Korea, and (to a lesser
extent) Brazil are outliers here. It is worth underlining the fact that in both

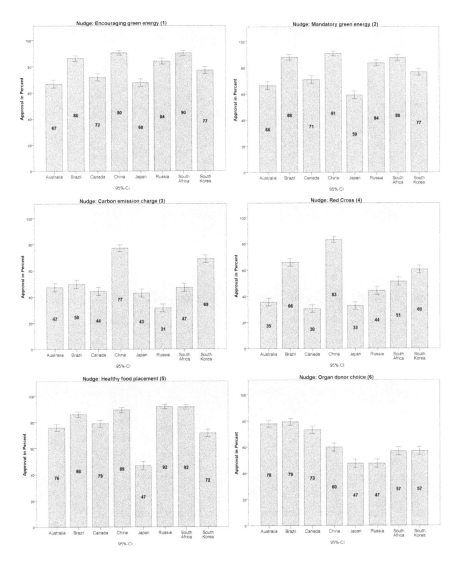

Figure 5.3 Mandatory default rules imposed by governments. CI, confidence
interval

China and South Korea, strong majorities favor default rules that are widely
disapproved in most other nations. Here is evidence against Hypothesis 2:
the unusually high approval ratings come from China and South Korea, not
China and Russia.

With respect to healthy food placement and active choosing for organ
donation, the picture is broadly consistent across nations. For healthy food

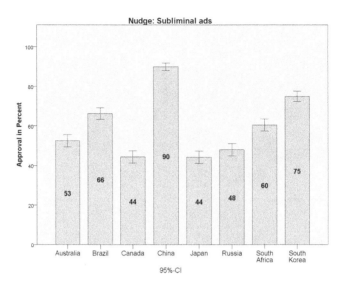

Figure 5.4 Mandatory subliminal advertising. CI, confidence interval

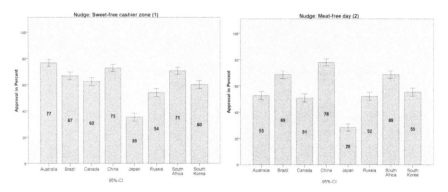

Figure 5.5 Mandatory choice architecture. CI, confidence interval

placement, Japan is yet again the evident outlier. For organ donation, China and South Korea show what is, for those nations, anomalously low approval ratings. Majorities disapprove in Russia as well as Japan. The Russian case is interesting and not simple to explain, though it is likely connected with identifiable (though to our knowledge not yet identified) aspects of the political and cultural backdrop.

As we have noted, previous work shows high levels of disapproval of subliminal advertising (along with significant support), even for what might seem to be a good cause, and the standard pattern is roughly observed in Canada, Japan, and Russia. One possible way to think about such data is that the minority approval rates (often in excess of 40 percent) represent the upper bound on the degree to which people will approve of violations of autonomy when the goals of the policy are deemed laudable.

But puzzlingly, and in a partial but important rejection of Hypothesis 1, we find overwhelmingly high approval rates in China and South Korea, and majority support as well in Australia, Brazil, and South Africa. We did not anticipate this result and are unsure how to explain it. One possibility is that the very idea of subliminal advertising is not perceived as especially troubling in those nations. Another possibility is that the public policy goals are taken to be sufficiently compelling as to justify the use of a presumptively unacceptable tool.

Sweet-free cashier zones and meat-free days produced strikingly similar patterns of results. The former—a kind of choice architecture designed to promote health—did obtain majority support in all nations except Japan, but with a significant spread between the highest rate (in Australia) and the lowest (in Russia). Meat-free days also obtained majority support in all nations with the exception of Japan, but here China was the most supportive and Australia the least.

Consistent with Hypothesis 1, the patterns that we observe here are similar to those found in Europe and the United States. With respect to sweet-free cashier zones, for example, Australia, China, and South Africa look a lot like Italy, France, and the United Kingdom. With respect to meat-free days, Italy and France are quite similar to Brazil, China, and South Africa.

Demographics and political attitude

We estimated the multilevel regression for each of the five levels of depth of intervention, with the approval rates of the 15 nudges being dependent variables. We calculated mean approval in percentages by level of intervention. Gender, age, educational level (in years of schooling), and political attitude (self-assessed) were used as independent variables on an individual level, and country on the country level. Results are presented in Table 5.1 and put into perspective below.

Notably, Table 5.1 shows that *gender* has a systematic influence on participants' approval of nudges: Women approve four out of five nudge types (2, 3, 4, 5) significantly more than men do. We would take this finding with some caution. Undoubtedly there are some nudges that would show the opposite pattern (nudges that encourage boxing, gambling, drinking,

Table 5.1 Estimates of selected socio-demographics and political attitude on nudge approval per nudge cluster: Multilevel analysis

Nudge clusters	(1) Information: Government campaigns	(2) Information: Governmentally mandated nudges	(3) Default rules	(4) Subliminal advertising	(5) Other mandates
Male	.281	−1.429**	−1.707**	−5.767***	−4.024***
	(.459)	(.531)	(.574)	(1.065)	(.862)
Age (in years)	.034*	.068***	−.060***	−.069*	.191***
	(.014)	(.017)	(.018)	(.034)	(.028)
School (in years)	.005	.179**	−.091	−.235*	−.037
	(.049)	(.057)	(.061)	(.114)	(.092)
Political attitude	−.008	−.448*	−.533*	1.544***	−.760*
(1= liberal to 7=conserv.)	(.186)	(.215)	(.233)	(.432)	(.350)
Obs.	7,594	7,594	7,594	7,594	7,594
ICC (intercept=country)	.024	.098	.118	.101	.112
P value intercept variance	(.056)	(.048)	(.047)	(.048)	(.047)

Legend: * $p \leq .05$; ** $p \leq .01$; *** $p \leq .001$.
Note: Estimates of a 2-level random intercept model. Standard errors in parentheses. Dependent variables are the average nudge groups by intrusiveness (Min: 0; Max: 100). The intraclass correlation coefficient (ICC) is the proportion of total variance that is attributed to the cluster "country".

and hunting?). If women are more supportive of the nudges tested here, it is probably because of the particular goals of those nudges.

The influence of *age* is strong but operates differently for different nudges. Older people tend to favor less intrusive interventions—such as information campaigns and information nudges that are mandated by the government—significantly more than younger people. Similarly, a meat-free day and sweet-free cashier zones are favored more strongly by older survey participants. At the same time, younger people are more likely than older people to approve of more intrusive interventions (such as manipulative messages and default rules). We would not make much of these findings.

Education (measured by school attendance in years) has a weaker influence, and it cuts in intriguingly different directions: The higher the number of years in school, the higher the approval level for governmentally mandated information nudges and the lower the approval level for subliminal advertising. It is plausible to speculate that more formally educated people are highly receptive to information as a regulatory tool; and they might be more skeptical of any use of government power to manipulate people.

A mixed picture emerges with respect to the influence of participants' self-assessed *political attitude*. As expected, acceptance for nudges rises with the grade of "liberalism" (meaning left-of-center) for three out of the five nudge types (2, 3, 5). Interestingly, the opposite is true for subliminal advertising, which is more likely to be supported by conservatives than by liberals. In general, and importantly, political attitudes have only a modest effect on approval rates, consistent with Chapters 2 and 4.

Three categories of nations

Hypothesis 1 is strongly supported (with a few qualifications). Overall, the level of approval of the presented nudges in our survey countries is generally high. The majority of respondents approve of most of the nudges in nearly all of the countries. In general, we find more similarities than differences among the surveyed countries. The same holds true when we compare the results with the US and European studies discussed in previous chapters.

There appears to be a large category of nations where majorities are likely to approve of nudges so long as they have legitimate ends and are consistent with the interests and values of most people. This, then, is the first of the three categories of nations that we are now in a position to describe: principled pro-nudge nations, where identifiable principles separate majority approval from majority disapproval.

The category of principled pro-nudge nations includes the industrialized Western democracies of our sample (Australia, Canada, France, Germany, Italy, the UK, the US), where we find exceptionally similar approval rates. Apparently such nations have similar norms and values, at least with respect to nudges. It may also be relevant that in much of the Anglo-Saxon world and in some of our sample countries in particular, nudges have been used and publicly debated for many years.

Russia, Brazil, and South Africa show broadly similar patterns, and with appropriate qualifications they can be placed in the same category as Western democracies. Of the three, Russia is the most surprising (and in partial rejection of both of our hypotheses). More research on the three nations would be necessary to explain the basic findings here.[9]

By contrast, the three Asian countries look very different. Contrary to our expectations, Japan is—like Denmark and Hungary in Europe—a clear outlier, with systematically and significantly lower approval rates than all other countries in 13 out of 15 cases. (The two exceptions are that Russians show higher disapproval rates of the carbon emission charge and that Canadians are more likely to disapprove of the Red Cross default donation.) In this light, it seems safe to say that a cluster of nations shows distinctly lower enthusiasm for nudges—and that in the fullness of time, we will have a clearer sense of which nations will join the category now containing Denmark, Hungary, and Japan. These are cautiously pro-nudge nations; there may turn out to be anti-nudge nations as well, though we have not yet found any.

It should also be possible to obtain a much clearer understanding of exactly why approval rates are lower in those nations. It is plausible to speculate that there is, in those nations, relatively less enthusiasm for the ends that the relevant nudges are designed to promote. If, for example, reducing smoking does not seem so important, then there will be less support for nudges that are designed to reduce smoking. We suspect that lower levels of enthusiasm for the relevant end do explain some of our findings. But with respect to Denmark, Hungary, and Japan, the more natural (though

9 There are some examples for interventions based on behavioral insights in these countries: According to the *Moscow Times*, Russia had planned the introduction of "traffic light" food labeling in 2017. Brazil adopted a law in 1997 regarding organ donor choice when getting the driver's license; however, the law was repealed in 1998 (http://news.bbc.co.uk/1/hi/health/7733190.stm).

also speculative) explanation points to reduced levels of trust in government. Many people might follow a kind of heuristic: *If the government plans to do it, it is probably a bad idea.* More systematic analysis would, of course, be necessary to test this explanation, and to understand why trust would be reduced in the relevant periods.

At the current time, there is only limited recent data on levels of confidence in government, and it does suggest that reduced levels do help to explain the data for Hungary in particular.[10] Also consistent with our findings, Japan's confidence in government level is slightly below the OECD average (yet rising since 2007),[11] but puzzlingly, Denmark sticks out—as do all Scandinavian countries—with high trust levels.[12] We attempt to make more progress on these issues in Chapter 6.

South Korea and China are also outliers, but in the other direction, generally showing overwhelmingly high approval rates for all nudges. It therefore seems safe to say that there is a third category of nations showing especially high enthusiasm for nudges, and therefore warranting the name of *overwhelmingly pro-nudge nations.*

We do not yet know how many nations fall into this category, nor do we know what accounts for their high levels of enthusiasm. A tempting though again speculative explanation, paralleling that just given, is that there is a consensus, in those nations, that particular nudges have compelling justifications—say, because of a widespread belief that distracted driving is a serious problem. Another explanation is that in those nations, trust in government is particularly high, so that strong majorities are inclined to support any policy, even if it is hypothetical. They follow a kind of heuristic: *If the government plans to do it, it is probably a good idea.* There is survey evidence that in China, levels of trust in government are indeed high and rising.[13] The Chinese

---

10 See OECD, "Confidence in National Government in 2014 and its Change since 2007" in *Government at a Glance 2015* (2015); OECD, *Trust and Public Policy: How Better Governance Can Help Rebuild Public Trust* (2017).

11 www.oecd.org/gov/GAAG2013_CFS_JPN.pdf.

12 See OECD, "Confidence in National Government in 2014 and its Change Since 2007" in *Government at a Glance 2015* (2015); OECD, *Trust and Public Policy: How Better Governance Can Help Rebuild Public Trust* (2017).

13 "The Chinese trust in their government has been rising steadily as Chinese perceive that their government is acting for their best interests—rather than for a privileged few" www.quora.com/Do-Chinese-citizens-trust-their-government (accessed February 20, 2017). See also Pew Research Center, Global Attitudes and Trends (www.pewglobal.org/2013/05/23/chapter-1-national-and-economic-conditions/). According to the Edelman Trust Barometer, trust percentage in government rose again in 2018; as a result,

people have high expectations that the state will raise living standards through direct control over investments and markets, and on average, living standards have improved markedly; the government has delivered in this respect.

We suspect, though we cannot prove, that these various explanations capture a large part of the picture—but not all of it. Begin with China, where approval rates tend to be highest of all. One reason could be that environmental issues in most of China are severe, and the adverse effects can be felt directly by the citizens, leading to general enthusiasm for nudges that involve the environment, health, or safety. Air pollution has received sustained attention in China, and during our field time, Premier Li publicly called for cleaner energy sources to adhere to the Paris Agreement; 23 Chinese cities had issued "red alerts" in December 2016 due to alarmingly unhealthy air pollution levels. It is also possible that Chinese people do indeed trust their government strongly and they genuinely approve most of its policies.

But it may also be relevant that in China, people are used to an authoritarian regime, run by the Chinese Communist Party, which intrudes on people's private decisions through mandates and bans (as, for example, through the one child policy and a recent plan to introduce a national smoking ban in public places). If mandates and bans are background facts, nudges might seem entirely unobjectionable.

Yet another possibility is that even though they were guaranteed anonymity, our respondents felt some pressure to declare support for the relevant policies. Consider the "Citizens Score," used by the Chinese government to classify its citizens into "good" or "bad" citizens; the existence of the score might act as a strong incentive to approve (online) everything the government plans.[14] In short, our results, showing stunningly high approval rates, might reflect a form of "preference falsification."[15]

What about South Korea? We did not expect to find the patterns there, and a full account would require a detailed investigation. The markedly high approval rates for most nudges might again be a product of enthusiasm for the policy

China ranks among the leading countries worldwide (www.forbes.com/sites/niallmccarthy/2018/01/22/the-countries-that-trust-their-government-most-and-least-infographic/#1ab14f79777a). We cannot, of course, exclude the possibility that these results are unreliable in a nation that is neither free nor democratic. For potential reasons and an academic discussion of this phenomenon—however from a decade ago—see Zhengxu Wang, Before the Emergence of Critical Citizens: Economic Development and Political Trust in China, Intl. Rev. of Soc. 15, 155 (2005).

14 www.aclu.org/blog/free-future/chinas-nightmarish-citizen-scores-are-warning-americans.
15 See Timur Kuran, Private Truths, Public Lies: The Social Consequences of Preference Falsification (1995).

goals and of general trust in government. In addition, there has been considerable discussion of nudging in the South Korean press. Though we did not use the term "nudge," and though we would not claim that press discussions are causal here, the idea of choice-preserving interventions, designed to promote health and safety goals, may well be familiar in the South Korean culture.

On the other hand, the high approval rates can be seen as surprising against the background of the two-month-long mass protests during our field time against the former President Park Geun-hye, who was accused of corruption. There was a threat of declaration of martial law to quell public protests. In the recent past, people in South Korea showed low levels of confidence in their government, and their suspicion with respect to corruption equaled that of Hungary.[16] Apparently public concerns about corruption, and about the current government, were insufficient to produce significant levels of disapproval of the kinds of policies tested here—a fact that may well attest to the deep cultural receptivity, in South Korea, to those policies.

Lessons

Studying diverse nations, we find strong majority support for nudges, with the important exception of Japan, and with spectacularly high approval rates in China and South Korea. The largest conclusion is that the nations of the world appear to fall into three groups: (1) a sizeable group of nations, mostly liberal democracies, where strong majorities approve of health and safety nudges; (2) a small group of nations where overwhelming majorities approve of nearly all nudges; and (3) a small group of nations where majorities generally support nudges, but where the level of support is markedly lower than in nations that fall in category (1).

With respect to cross-national differences, much remains to be learned and our explanations have been tentative and speculative; this is an important domain for further work and for the development of testable hypotheses. For example, we do not know whether the very high levels of support in China reflect trust in government, enthusiasm about the policy goals, adaptation to the extensive use of government power, or some form of "preference falsification," producing misleadingly high levels of support in surveys.

Nor do we know, as yet, whether many countries fall within the category of overwhelmingly pro-nudge nations, now containing only China

16 See OECD, "Confidence in National Government in 2014 and its Change since 2007" in *Government at a Glance 2015* (2015).

and South Korea, or whether the category of more cautiously pro-nudge nations is small and greatly dominated, in terms of sheer numbers, by the principled pro-nudge consensus among democratic nations (as now appears). It also remains possible that some nations would show only minority support for the nudges tested here.

We have speculated that for Hungary and Japan, a lack of trust in government is a significant part of the picture. It would be parsimonious to show that trust, across nations and across time, provides the principal explanation of cross-national differences. We now turn to that question.

Appendix to Chapter 5

Table A5.1 Observations RIM weighted/unweighted for all countries

Country	Weighted sample		Unweighted sample	
	Frequency	Percent	Frequency	Percent
Australia	1,000	12.5	1,001	12.6
Brazil	1,000	12.5	1,000	12.6
Canada	1,000	12.5	1,137	14.3
China	1,000	12.5	985	12.4
Japan	1,000	12.5	1,005	12.7
Russia	1,000	12.5	918	11.6
South Africa	1,000	12.5	949	12.0
South Korea	1,000	12.5	932	11.8
Total	8,000	100.0	7,927	100.0

Note: For each country, we predefined country-specific quotas for socio-demographic variables on the basis of the respective national census data to be reached in the sampling. In Australia, Brazil, Canada, and Japan, quotas for age, gender, and region could be reached. In China, Russia, South Africa, and South Korea, it turned out to be impossible to recruit the needed numbers of low-educated respondents—which is not so surprising in light of the fact that we used a web-based instrument. After several extensions of field time, we had to loosen the quotas for education in all countries. To make up for this shortcoming, we used oversampling and weighting. To ensure representativeness with respect to gender, age, region, and education for China, Russia, South Africa, and South Korea, RIM weighting was conducted. The same procedure was conducted for the samples of Australia, Brazil, Canada, and Japan (which were already representative with respect to age, gender, and region) in order to ensure representative results regarding education levels.

6

TRUSTING NUDGES

In this chapter, we dig deeper. We seek to understand the differences among nations in more detail. We focus above all on the question of trust.

To do that digging, we collected additional data in four of our study countries (Germany, Denmark, South Korea, and the US) in 2018.[1] We chose one nation from each of the three categories of nudge endorsement and one from each of three different cultural clusters. We also added comparable survey data from Belgium (Flanders).[2] In addition to the 15 nudges and the socio-demographic variables, we asked participants to answer a large questionnaire including anthropometrics (to calculate Body Mass Index), lifestyle factors, consumption of specific products (alcohol, smoking, and meat), employment status and type, subjective health status and health satisfaction, social trust and trust in institutions, concerns about the environment, world-views and thinking styles (i.e., future outlook, belief

---

1 An earlier version of this chapter was published as Cass R. Sunstein, Lucia A. Reisch and Micha Kaiser (forthcoming), Trusting Nudges? Lessons from An International Survey, *Journal of European Public Policy*, www.tandfonline.com/doi/full/10.1080.13501763.2018.1531912.

2 This data has been provided by the Flemish government that followed our survey procedure. For Flemish results see: Veerle Beyst and Kristof Rubens (2018), *Wordt "nudging" in het beleid aanvaard in Vlaanderen?*, VTOM 2018/4, pp. 53–65.

in free markets, political attitudes, risk aversion), and several additional variables. We speculated that these variables could help explain differences between social groups as well as across nations.

Above all, we were interested in the psychological concepts of social and institutional trust. These concepts have since long been depicted as important indicators of the strength and quality of societies, communities, and governments across the world. Validated measurement items as well as prevalence estimates are available for most countries worldwide—for instance, from the World Values Survey data set.[3] In our study, we hypothesized that people who have a high trust in public institutions would be more willing to accept government nudging in our tested areas. We also speculated that strong believers in the free market might be less inclined to do so.

We also tested other variables. The influence of environmental concern on attitudes and behavior has been studied in depth and in international contexts.[4] It seems intuitive that people who have a marked concern regarding the environment[5] will endorse environmental policies in general and "green nudges" specifically.[6] As expected, this is what we found. For similar reasons, we speculated that a fragile individual health status and high health concerns for oneself and others might be positively correlated with approval of health nudges. A recent study[7] reported that a higher Body Mass Index (BMI) was positively correlated with support for menu labelling policies (which is Nudge 1 in our list of 15 nudges). We also explored the influence of consumption habits (i.e., meat, tobacco, alcohol, and mobility) on the approval of the respective nudges.

---

3 See Ronald Inglehart et al. (eds.), *World Values Survey: Round Six—Country-Pooled* (2014). Data-file Version: www.worldvaluessurvey.org/WVSDocumentationWV6.jsp. Social trust was measured by the questions from the World Values Survey (WVS): "Would you say that most people can be trusted?" and "How much do you trust people from the following various groups".

4 E.g., A. Franzen and D. Vogl, 2013, Two Decades of Measuring Environmental Attitudes: A Comparative Analysis of 33 Countries, *Global Environmental Change* 23(5), 1001–8; Wouter Poortinga, Linda Steg, and Charles Vlek (2004), Values, Environmental Concern, and Environmental Behavior: A Study into Household Energy Use, *Environment and Behavior* 36(1), 70–93.

5 Measured by the question: "How much are you concerned about the environment?".

6 Note that the aim of this research was not to compare the approval of different policy tools such as legislation, taxes, or behavioral nudges, nor the different ways nudges are framed, e.g., as win or loss. Other studies have done that.

7 J. Bhawra, J. L. Reid, and C. M. White et al. (2018), Are Young Canadians Supportive of Proposed Nutrition Policies and Regulations? An Overview of Policy Support and the Impact of Socio-demographic Factors on Public Opinion, *Canadian Journal of Public Health*.

As before, we were also interested whether approval rates of nudging depend on political attitudes of people. As we saw in Chapter 2, Republicans in the United States show somewhat lower approval rates for some nudges than do Democrats. However, this could well be due to the choice of policy domains; recall "partisan nudge bias." In earlier chapters, we found no systematic correlation along approval and party affiliations. Finally, we speculated that risk aversion, job satisfaction, and subjective well-being might have an impact on approval.

In brief: With this study, we aimed to understand *why* people in selected countries approve or disapprove of a set of 15 nudges, mainly in the field of environmental protection and health. Regarding explanatory variables, our principal focus is on trust in governmental institutions. Further, by replicating the surveys in earlier chapters, we test the robustness of our earlier results regarding approval rates and socio-demographics, in particular the influence of gender. And by compiling all available data on nudge approval rates from the three waves in 16 countries (as far as methodologically possible), we hope to shed broader light on public acceptance of nudges.

The remainder of this chapter is organized as follows. We first present the methodology of the study by describing the samples, the survey, the variables, as well as the multi-step statistical analysis. We then show the results in the five countries (Belgium, Denmark, Germany, South Korea, and the US), emphasizing above all the relationship between the trust variables and approval rates. We also compare the present results with earlier survey waves in selected countries and provide an overall view of all surveys of all our respective empirical studies. We discuss the results and limitations of our study and conclude with comments on implications for nudging research and behavioral public policy. Our ultimate emphasis, based on our findings about trust, involve the importance of public participation and consultation with respect to behaviorally informed policies.

The study

Sampling and survey

We employed an online representative survey in five countries representing different levels of overall nudge approval as sketched in Chapter 5: The US and Germany (principled pro-nudge nations), South Korea (overwhelmingly pro-nudge), and Denmark (cautiously pro-nudge). As a new country in our database, we included (the Flemish part of) Belgium.[8] Again, we employed the market research company Qualtrics[9] to conduct the survey. Field time was during six weeks in January and February 2018. We had permanent access to the survey data and could monitor the survey and the fulfilment of quota on a daily basis. Table A6.1 in the appendix provides an overview of the different samples and sampling of this survey.

Survey instrument

We employed a questionnaire with 53 questions including socio-demographic variables; the list of 15 nudges in a randomized order as employed in our earlier studies; a measure of political attitudes; questions measuring psychological constructs (such as social trust and trust in government, perceived freedom of choice) as well as variables describing individual factors (such as perceived individual health, environmental concern, social trust as well as consumption practices, such as smoking and drinking habits). The complete survey instrument, as the descriptive statistics of the underlying data set, and the full list of variables employed have been published elsewhere.[10]

As before: The questionnaire was fully structured, and respondents were required to follow them as provided. Each item was shown on a single screen. Answering categories were adapted to the respective questions and ranged from Likert scales to binary schemes. Except for the socio-demographic questions, all items were randomized. As in all earlier surveys, respondents were prompted with the question "Do you approve or disprove of the following hypothetical policy?" The answer categories were "approve" or "disapprove."

With respect to "trust in institutions," we used two different questions to reduce the risk of methodological artifacts. The first was taken from the World Value Survey: "How much do you trust in the following institutions?" Then a set of public institutions was listed (namely: the armed forces; the police; the courts; the government; political parties; parliament;

---

8 To ensure the same approach and level of quality of the Flemish sampling and survey processes (and later on, the Mexican study), we developed a Standard Operation Procedure on how to run our survey; it is available from the authors on request.

9 www.qualtrics.com.

10 See Appendix A1 and A2 respectively in Cass R. Sunstein, Lucia A. Reisch and Micha Kaiser (forthcoming), *Trusting Nudges?, supra* note 1.

the civil service; universities; the European Union; the United Nations). The second item asked: "How much do you trust governmental institutions?" We also asked whether people believe in the free market as the best way to solve environmental and economic problems, a question used in environmental research. All items were to be answered on a seven-point Likert scale.

As in previous surveys, statistical equivalence of the questionnaire was ensured by professional translation of the new questionnaire items from English in the respective languages, followed by a back-translation into English. The Flemish questionnaire was translated, back-translated, and adapted in full. Due to the high internet penetration rates in the covered countries, we could assume that answers were not systematically skewed due to lack of internet access or proficiency.

Statistical analysis

The statistical analysis took place in several steps and with several methodological approaches. (In the present chapter, we report only on the main results.) In a first step, in order to get an overview of whether and how this large number of variables (23) were interlinked, we drew a correlation heatmap indicating correlations among all variables (Figure 6.1). On the basis of the heatmap, we selected obviously correlating variables as identified by the map and looked into those more in depth. We then undertook a multilevel regression of all variables and nudge approval (Table 6.1), tested the robustness of the results with the help of a decision tree analysis, and estimated the size of the probabilities. For the regressions and the machine learning algorithms, the 15 nudges were categorized in five nudge clusters as used in Chapter 5.

Results

Nudge approval, trust, and selected variables

The correlation heatmap as shown in Figure 6.1 suggests some expected descriptive correlations between nudge approval and relevant variables.

As in prior studies, gender and age showed significant correlations with approval. Moreover, the new variables "trust in institutions" and "environmental concern" were found to correlate strongly with higher nudge

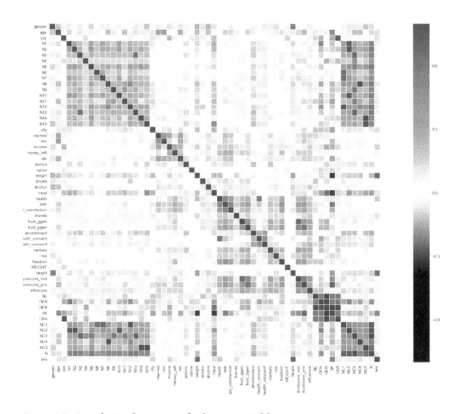

Figure 6.1 Correlation heatmap of relevant variables
Note: To download this figure in color please visit the e-resource at www.routledge.
com/9781138322783.

approval. "Belief in markets" was correlated with lower approval. Approval
rates by gender, conditional on trust in institutions (trustscore_inst), are
depicted in Figure 6.2. As shown, higher trust in institutions seems to be
linked to higher approval on average, and more so for women than for
men.

Interestingly, the concepts "social trust" and "trust in other people"
were not correlated with approval rates. But that is not entirely surprising;
our focus is on *governmental* policies, and higher trust in institutions is the
more relevant question. Furthermore, and perhaps surprisingly, the heatmap did not suggest strong and significant correlations between overall
nudge approval and a large set of variables, notably health status and health
concern for oneself, subjective well-being, perceived freedom of choice,
risk aversion, and BMI.

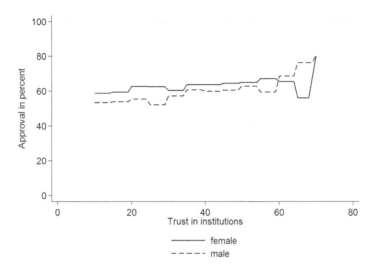

Figure 6.2 Overall nudge approval, conditional on trust in institutions

Note: The graph uses the World Wide Survey Question "On a scale of 1 to 7: How much do you trust the following (10) institutions" as explanatory variable (*trustscore_inst*).

At the same time, the map does suggest some expected results. Meat consumption seems to be negatively correlated with approval of "a meat-free day in public canteens" (Nudge 15); smokers disapprove of government campaigns (and subliminal advertising) against smoking (Nudge 12), and people who drink alcohol more frequently disapprove of nudging in general. To that extent, behavior seems to play a role; people do not want to be nudged to stop doing something that they like to do, and are now doing. In a way, that should not be surprising, but it might have been predicted that people engaging in harmful behavior (such as smoking) might be especially supportive of efforts to reduce that behavior.

Trust in institutions

The relationship between trust in institutions and nudge approval was confirmed by weighted regression, where the effects were strong and significant. As expected, we also found a significant negative relationship between "belief in markets" and nudge approval. (Note parenthetically that we might have tested nudges that promote reliance on markets, in which case the relationship would be expected to be positive.) Column (1) in Table 6.1 shows the regression results for all nudges together as well as for the five nudge clusters.

Table 6.1 Weighted OLS regression for different nudge clusters (2018 survey)

	Clusters					
	(1)	(2)	(3)	(4)	(5)	(6)
	Overall approval	Government campaigns	Information nudges	Default rules	Subliminal ads	Other mandates
GER	0.0316***	0.0165	0.0494***	−0.0169	0.0986***	0.1394***
	(0.012)	(0.014)	(0.015)	(0.014)	(0.025)	(0.020)
DEN	−0.0689***	−0.0800***	−0.1041***	−0.0776***	−0.0540**	0.0193
	(0.011)	(0.014)	(0.017)	(0.014)	(0.024)	(0.020)
KOREA	0.1390***	0.1289***	0.1961***	0.1257***	0.3433***	0.0064
	(0.014)	(0.017)	(0.018)	(0.018)	(0.031)	(0.027)
BE	0.0413***	0.0334**	0.0219	0.0046	0.1728***	0.1267***
	(0.011)	(0.014)	(0.016)	(0.014)	(0.024)	(0.020)
Male	−0.0188***	−0.0130	−0.0169*	−0.0104	−0.0124	−0.0590***
	(0.007)	(0.009)	(0.010)	(0.009)	(0.016)	(0.013)
Age	−0.0006**	0.0007**	−0.0000	−0.0014***	−0.0024***	−0.0004
	(0.000)	(0.000)	(0.000)	(0.000)	(0.001)	(0.000)
Yos	−0.0032***	−0.0015	−0.0031***	−0.0034***	−0.0060***	−0.0040***
	(0.001)	(0.001)	(0.001)	(0.001)	(0.002)	(0.001)
City	0.0045**	0.0052*	0.0068**	0.0036	0.0079	0.0011
	(0.002)	(0.003)	(0.003)	(0.003)	(0.005)	(0.004)
Married	0.0055	0.0065	−0.0053	0.0053	0.0162	0.0154
	(0.008)	(0.010)	(0.011)	(0.010)	(0.019)	(0.014)
Noc	0.0060*	0.0003	0.0022	0.0082**	−0.0003	0.0165***
	(0.003)	(0.004)	(0.004)	(0.004)	(0.007)	(0.006)
Income	−0.0015	−0.0005	0.0009	−0.0036**	−0.0038	0.0009
	(0.001)	(0.001)	(0.002)	(0.001)	(0.003)	(0.002)
Money left	0.0000	0.0077	0.0127	−0.0142	0.0215	0.0012
	(0.008)	(0.009)	(0.010)	(0.009)	(0.016)	(0.013)
Car	0.0047	−0.0086	0.0198	0.0011	0.0079	0.0116
	(0.009)	(0.011)	(0.012)	(0.011)	(0.019)	(0.015)
Politics	−0.0053**	−0.0068**	−0.0047	−0.0065**	0.0088	−0.0077*
	(0.002)	(0.003)	(0.003)	(0.003)	(0.005)	(0.004)
Native	−0.0349***	−0.0200	−0.0361**	−0.0219	−0.0824***	−0.0705***
	(0.012)	(0.015)	(0.016)	(0.015)	(0.028)	(0.019)
Smoke	−0.0100	−0.0331***	−0.0102	0.0133	−0.0749***	−0.0122
	(0.008)	(0.009)	(0.010)	(0.010)	(0.017)	(0.014)

(Continued)

			Clusters			
	(1)	(2)	(3)	(4)	(5)	(6)
	Overall approval	Government campaigns	Information nudges	Default rules	Subliminal ads	Other mandates
Alcohol	−0.0092***	−0.0101**	−0.0152***	−0.0085**	−0.0032	−0.0038
	(0.003)	(0.004)	(0.004)	(0.004)	(0.007)	(0.006)
Meat	−0.0120***	0.0054	−0.0087*	−0.0102**	−0.0128*	−0.0481***
	(0.004)	(0.004)	(0.005)	(0.004)	(0.008)	(0.006)
Health	0.0007	0.0075*	−0.0040	−0.0021	0.0146**	−0.0009
	(0.003)	(0.004)	(0.004)	(0.004)	(0.007)	(0.006)
Swb	−0.0057	−0.0092**	−0.0037	−0.0059	0.0003	−0.0057
	(0.003)	(0.004)	(0.005)	(0.004)	(0.008)	(0.006)

Notes: "Yos" means "years of schooling". "Noc" means "number of children". "Swb" means "subjective well-being".

Trust in institutions is highly correlated with approval of nudges. To predict marginal probabilities of nudge approval, i.e., the predicted size of the effects, we estimated a logistic model for each nudge question as independent variable separately. Predicted marginal probabilities for approval conditioned on institutional trust—as shown in Figure 6.3—differ substantially between the lowest possible trust score (10) and the highest possible trust score (70). For instance, while (ceteris paribus) the probability to accept the nudge "Encouraging green energy" (Nudge 3) is estimated to be around 55 percent for individuals with the lowest possible value of institutional trust (for an average individual in the sample), this probability increases to almost 95 percent for the highest trust value.

Further results

The same is true of environmental concern: results are strong, as expected. Other results from the regression analysis are worth reporting, though they are less significant. A higher formal education (years of schooling) is correlated with lower approval rates toward nudges on average. City dwellers tend to approve the tested nudges more than people who live in villages or in the countryside. The number of children is positively correlated with approval rates. Those who are left-of-center seem to approve of the tested nudges more than conservatives do.

Revisiting our categorization of countries regarding nudge approval we compiled the results from the three study waves (2015, 2016, and 2017/18), including 16 countries. Table A6.3 in the appendix gives an overview of samples and sampling in all countries, with an overall N of 20,501 respondents. We used the comparable data from these surveys (we lacked some data from Mexico and Ireland, and also the US was not fully comparable) to run another regression analysis. Table A6.4 in the appendix shows the weighed OLS regression for the five nudge clusters. Confirming earlier results, the gender factor was again found to be highly relevant for nudge approval in each of the countries—except for China, where male respondents significantly approve of the tested nudges more than women (this is also visible in Figure A6.1 in the appendix). However, this should be interpreted in light of extremely high approval in China from both genders, with rates between 80 and 90 percent.

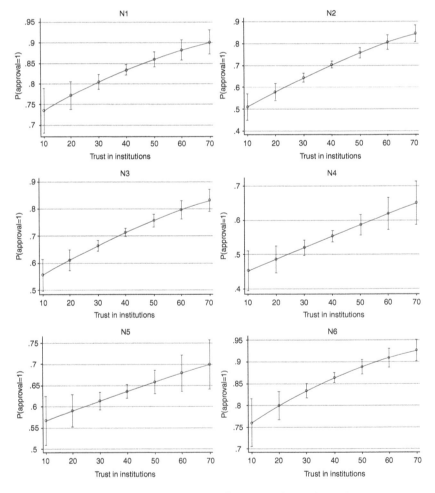

Figure 6.3 Predicted marginal probabilities for approval, conditional on
institutional trust

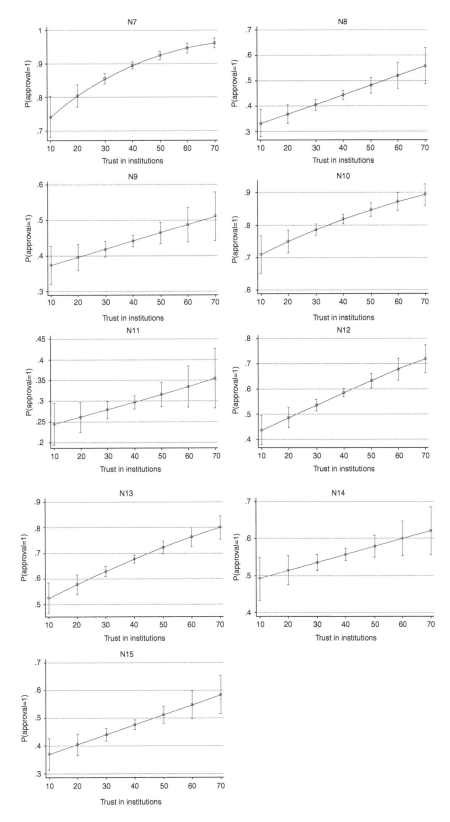

Figure 6.3 (Continued)

We also compared approval rates of the 15 nudges over time in Denmark, Germany, and South Korea—the three countries that we had revisited two and a half years after the first survey. Overall, approval rates in these countries were largely stable as compared to our earlier studies. We found only small changes in magnitude between those waves, with modest changes in both directions, i.e., less and more approval by both genders (Figure A6.2 in the appendix). The country categorizations—Denmark as a "cautiously pro-nudge country," Germany as a "principled pro-nudge nation," and South Korea as "overwhelmingly pro-nudge" (as explained in Chapter 5)—still applied three years later. This is particularly notable for the latter, since the country has undergone a marked democratization process in these past three years. Finally, the three countries that followed our methodology to measure their national nudge approval rate—namely Mexico, Ireland, and Belgium—turned out to be "overwhelmingly pro-nudge" (in the case of Mexico) and "principled pro-nudge nations" (in the cases of Belgium and Ireland).

Discussion

In some countries, policymakers have learned to tread around behavioral interventions with caution, in order to avoid being accused of being "national nannies" or even worse, of manipulating their citizens. Policy measures that lack public endorsement may well turn out to be less likely to succeed and to induce the intended behavioral changes without major unintended side effects. There are also questions about legitimacy, in the normative as well as the descriptive sense (see Chapter 9).

As in earlier studies, we have found general approval of nudges alongside marked national differences in levels of support, with Denmark on the least positive side, South Korea and Mexico the most positive, and Germany, Belgium, Ireland, and the US somewhere in between. As expected, support generally seems to decrease as the level of state intervention increases, as estimated along our five "nudge clusters" of levels of intrusion. (We would take this finding with caution in view of two facts: (1) much turns on the substance of the nudge, that is, the direction in which people are being nudged, rather than the level of intrusiveness; and (2) consistent with (1), people will approve of high levels of intrusion for egregious kinds of misconduct, e.g., murder, rape, assault, and theft.) In addition, approval is generally higher (or disapproval is lower) for those nudges that are targeted to others—i.e., businesses—and lower for those that target people directly. (We would also take this finding with caution. Many nudges applied to people directly receive high levels of approval; consider calorie labels. At the same time, some nudges applied to others would not receive approval; consider a nudge designed to increase air pollution.) Those who engage in the activity being nudged (e.g., smoking) are less likely to be supportive.

Our particular interest lay in the hypothesis that higher trust in public institutions will be correlated with stronger support of nudges. This has been confirmed. At the same time, people who believe in markets as the best institution to solve environmental and economic problems are more critical of nudges. Female gender was again found to be correlated with approval of the tested nudges. Further, people's own health concern and health status had no influence on acceptance, and meat consumption only on the (non)acceptance of the Nudge "meat-free days in cafeterias." The fact that approval rates in earlier tested countries have barely changed in the past three years is noteworthy, particularly in the case of South Korea where profound political changes have taken place.

For policymakers, our results convey relevant insights. Trust in public institutions in general and environmental concern might be useful allies in communicating about nudging and nudges. Endorsement of nudges in general might increase when citizens are invited to participate, actively choose, and offer feedback on planned interventions.[11] If they can be expected or reported, beneficial results in specific domains (health, environment, and safety) or with respect to specific consumption habits (meat, alcohol, or smoking) might be helpful in communicating with the public.

For purposes of both effectiveness and legitimacy, close engagement with the public and attentiveness to its concerns can be exceedingly important. It has been urged that a "one-nudge-fits-all" approach to behavioral public policy is unlikely to be successful.[12] Effective nudges, capable of receiving public acceptance, will more likely be developed with a process that includes early participation of the affected groups, public scrutiny, and deliberation—as well as transparent processes in governmental institutions.

11 See Peter John, How Far to Nudge? Assessing Behavioural Public Policy (2018).
12 See, e.g., OECD, Behavioural Insights and Public Policy: Lessons from Around the World (2018). See also Xavier Troussard and René van Bavel, How Can Behavioural Insights be Used to Improve EU Policy?, Intereconomics 53, 8 (2018).

In addition to public participation, the "test-learn-adapt-share" approach called for by leading policy labs worldwide is a prerequisite for success.[13]

We offer four points by way of conclusion. First, we have confirmed high levels of approval for nudges as policy tools across different countries and cultures. Second, Belgium and Ireland join the large set of democratic nations whose citizens generally embrace nudging, but with important exceptions and qualifications; Mexico looks more like China and South Korea, with overwhelmingly high approval rates. Third, levels of public acceptance are reduced as nudges become more intrusive. Fourth, trust in government institutions is highly correlated with approval of nudges.

We underline the last point. The best way to obtain trust is to earn it. In that light, it is important not only to ensure that behaviorally informed policies promote social welfare, but also to develop processes to ensure that such polices are adopted transparently, with ample opportunity for public engagement, and with openness to citizens' objections and concerns.

Appendix to Chapter 6

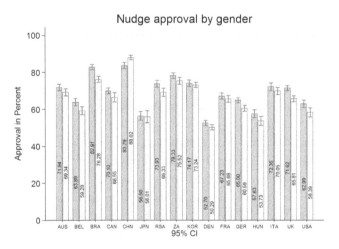

Figure A6.1 Nudge approval by gender (all studies)
Note: White shading indicates average male approval.

13 See, e.g., Laura Haynes et al., *Test, Learn, Adapt: Developing Public Policy with Randomised Controlled Trials*. Cabinet Office Behavioural Insights Team (2014); Joana Sousa Lourenco, Emanuele Ciriolo, Sara Rafael Rodrigues Vieira de Almeida and Xavier Troussard, *Behavioural Insights Applied to Policy*. Report No. EUR 27726 EN (2016).

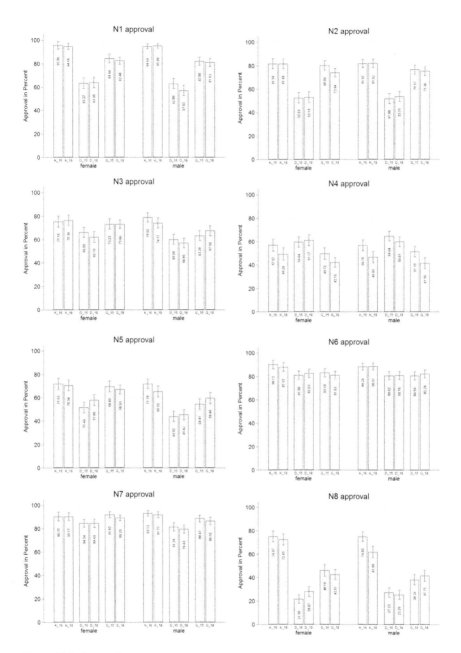

Figure A6.1 (Continued)

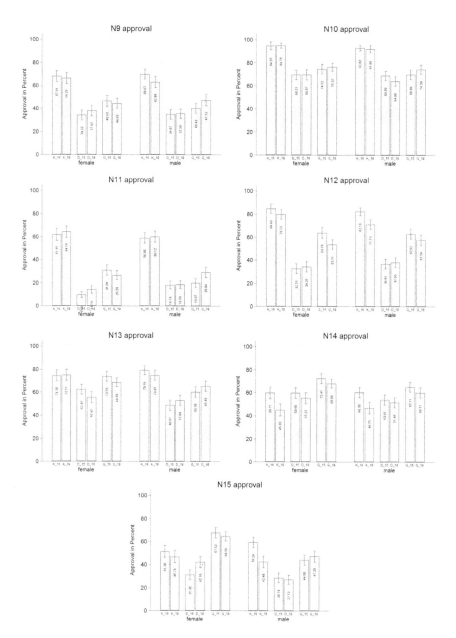

Figure A6.2 Nudge approval among different time periods for South Korea (K), Denmark (DK), and Germany (G)

Table A6.1 Samples and sampling in the different countries (2018 study): Types of representativeness and methodology (2018 survey)

Country	Data provider	Sample year	Unmodified sample size	Representativeness	Survey method	Weighting method	Sample	Recruiting for the panel	Census/ Population	Frame of the survey
Belgium	GfK	2017/2018	1,002	Online representative for gender, age, region and education	CAWI	No weighting	Quota sampling	Online	10 mio internet users, 18+ years	No frames
Denmark	Qualtrics	2017/2018	966	Online representative for gender, age, region and education	CAWI	RIM	Quota sampling	Online	5.4 mio internet users, 18+ years	No frames
Germany	Qualtrics	2017/2018	1,535	Online representative for gender, age, region and education	CAWI	RIM	Quota sampling	Online	55 mio internet users, 18+ years	No frames
South Korea	Qualtrics	2017/2018	1,017	Online representative for gender, age, region and education	CAWI	RIM	Quota sampling	Online	43.9 mio internet users, 18+ years	No frames
USA	Qualtrics	2017/2018	1,012	Online representative for gender, age, region and education	CAWI	RIM	Quota sampling	Online	272.4 mio internet users, 18+ years	No frames

Note: "Mio" means million.

Table A6.2 Descriptive statistics—all variables (2018 survey)

	N	μ	σ
Country	5,385.000	2.889	1.386
Gender	5,385.000	0.505	0.500
Age	5,385.000	46.676	16.391
Yos	5,385.000	12.297	4.989
N1	5,385.000	0.789	0.408
N2	5,385.000	0.668	0.471
N3	5,385.000	0.683	0.465
N4	5,385.000	0.537	0.499
N5	5,385.000	0.615	0.487
N6	5,385.000	0.843	0.364
N7	5,385.000	0.864	0.343
N8	5,385.000	0.429	0.495
N9	5,385.000	0.425	0.494
N10	5,385.000	0.777	0.416
N11	5,385.000	0.301	0.459
N12	5,385.000	0.558	0.497
N13	5,385.000	0.651	0.477
N14	5,385.000	0.542	0.498
N15	5,385.000	0.460	0.498
City	5,385.000	3.124	1.575
Married	5,385.000	0.480	0.500
Noc	5,385.000	1.179	1.250
Income	5,385.000	5.574	3.241
money_left	5,385.000	0.584	0.493
Car	5,385.000	0.753	0.431
Politics	5,385.000	3.945	1.360
Native	5,385.000	0.904	0.295
Weight	5,385.000	77.603	19.720
Smoke	5,385.000	0.286	0.452
Alcohol	5,385.000	1.949	1.070
Meat	5,385.000	3.342	1.110
Health	5,385.000	4.826	1.315
Swb	5,385.000	4.882	1.397
job_satisfaction	5,385.000	4.552	1.887
Friends	5,385.000	0.776	0.417

	N	μ	σ
trust_ggen	5,385.000	3.490	1.517
trust_pgen	5,385.000	4.101	1.322
Environment	5,385.000	4.940	1.439
health_concern	5,385.000	4.479	1.570
health_concernf	5,385.000	4.595	1.505
Markets	5,385.000	3.958	1.414
Risk	5,385.000	3.795	1.435
Freedom	5,385.000	5.012	1.374
Height	5,385.000	171.425	9.661
trustscore_inst	5,385.000	37.462	12.162
trustscore_priv	5,385.000	25.926	6.493
Infoscore	5,385.000	23.866	7.278
N	5,385.000	0.609	0.235
NC1	5,385.000	0.755	0.282
NC2	5,385.000	0.745	0.325
NC3	5,385.000	0.535	0.283
NC4	5,385.000	0.429	0.495
NC5	5,385.000	0.501	0.400
BMI	5,385.000	26.307	6.003

Notes: "Yos" means "years of schooling". "Noc" means "number of children". "Swb" means "subjective well-being". "Trust_ggen" means "trust in government, in general". "Trust_pgen" means "trust in people, in general". "Health_concernf'" means "concern about the future health status of friends and relatives".

Table A6.3 Samples and sampling in the different countries: Types of representativeness and methodology (16 countries, all samples, all waves)

Country	Data provider	Sample year	Unmodified sample size	Representativeness	Survey method	Weighting method	Sample	Recruiting for the panel	Census/ Population	Frame of the survey
Australia	Qualtrics	2016	1,001	Online representative for gender, age, region and education	CAWI	Target	Quota sampling	Online	21 mio internet users, 18+ years	No frames
Belgium	GfK	2017/2018	1,002	Online representative for gender, age, region and education	CAWI	No weighting	Quota sampling	Online	10 mio internet users, 18+ years	No frames
Brazil	Qualtrics	2016	1,000	Online representative for gender, age, region and education	CAWI	Target	Quota sampling	Online	93 mio internet users, 18+ years	No frames
Canada	Qualtrics	2016	1,137	Online representative for gender, age, region and education	CAWI	Target	Quota sampling	Online	29.5 mio internet users, 18+ years	No frames
China	Qualtrics	2016	985	Online representative for gender, age, region and education	CAWI	Target	Quota sampling	Online	533 mio internet users, 18+ years	No frames
Denmark	Qualtrics	2017/2018	966	Online representative for gender, age, region and education	CAWI	RIM	Quota sampling	Online	5.4 mio internet users, 18+ years	No frames

Country	Provider	Year	Sample	Representativeness	Mode	Weighting	Sampling	Online/Offline	Population	Topic
Denmark	GfK	2015	1,000	F2f representative for gender, age, region	CAWI omnibus	Target	Quota sampling	Offline	4.54 mio internet users, 18+ years	About consumer goods (soft drinks, coffee machines, hearing aids) and crossing the Great Belt Bridge
France	GfK	2015	1,022	F2f representative for gender, age, region	CAWI omnibus	Target	Quota sampling	Online	41.05 mio (population of 16–64 years)	About views on the Ukraine
Germany	Qualtrics	2017/2018	1,535	Online representative for gender, age, region and education	CAWI	RIM	Quota sampling	Online	55 mio internet users, 18+ years	No frames
Germany	GfK	2015	1,012	Online representative for gender, age, region	CAWI omnibus	RIM	Quota sampling	Offline and online	55.06 mio internet users, 14+ years	About views on the economy
Hungary	GfK	2015	1,001	F2f representative for gender, age, region	CAWI omnibus	RIM	Quota sampling	Offline	7.35 mio, 15–69 years	Ad hoc, no other frames
Italy	GfK	2015	1,011	Online representative for gender, age, region	CAWI omnibus	No weighting	Quota sampling	Offline and online	35 mio internet users, 18–64 years	No frames
Japan	Qualtrics	2016	1005	Online representative for gender, age, region and education	CAWI	Target	Quota sampling	Online	99 mio internet users, 18+ years	No frames

(Continued)

Country	Data provider	Sample year	Unmodified sample size	Representativeness	Survey method	Weighting method	Sample	Recruiting for the panel	Casus/ Population	Frame of the survey
Russia	Qualtrics	2016	918	Online representative for gender, age, region and education	CAWI	Target	Quota sampling	Online	70 mio internet users, 18+ years	No frames
South Africa	Qualtrics	2016	949	Online representative for gender, age, region and education	CAWI	Target	Quota sampling	Online	43.9 mio internet users, 18+ years	No frames
South Korea	Qualtrics	2017/2018	1,017	Online representative for gender, age, region and education	CAWI	RIM	Quota sampling	Online	43.9 mio internet users, 18+ years	No frames
South Korea	Qualtrics	2016	932	Online representative for gender, age, region and education	CAWI	Target	Quota sampling	Online	11 mio internet users, 18+ years	No frames
UK	GfK	2015	2,033	F2f representative for gender, age, region	CAWI omni-bus	RIM	Quota sampling	Online	50.9 mio internet users, 18+ years	About saving and spending habits
USA	Qualtrics	2017/2018	1,012	Online representative for gender, age, region and education	CAWI	RIM	Quota sampling	Online	272.4 mio internet users, 18+ years	No frames

Note: "Mio" means million.

Table A6.4 Weighted OLS regression for different nudge clusters

	(1)	(2)	(3)	(4)	(5)	(6)
			Clusters			
	Overall approval	Government campaigns	Information nudges	Default rules	Subliminal ads	Other mandates
Male	−0.0304***	−0.0133***	−0.0240***	−0.0266***	−0.0544***	−0.0653***
	(0.003)	(0.004)	(0.005)	(0.004)	(0.008)	(0.006)
Age	−0.0002	0.0008***	0.0004***	−0.0011***	−0.0013***	0.0009***
	(0.000)	(0.000)	(0.000)	(0.000)	(0.000)	(0.000)
Higher education	−0.0108***	0.0065	−0.0022	−0.0192***	−0.0563***	−0.0015
	(0.004)	(0.005)	(0.005)	(0.005)	(0.009)	(0.007)
Belgium	−0.0720***	−0.0508***	−0.1186***	−0.0780***	−0.0090	−0.0479**
	(0.012)	(0.014)	(0.016)	(0.015)	(0.026)	(0.020)
Brazil	0.0908***	0.0643***	0.0427***	0.1394***	0.1392***	0.0326*
	(0.009)	(0.010)	(0.011)	(0.012)	(0.023)	(0.017)
Canada	−0.0218**	−0.0137	−0.0205	0.0029	−0.0756***	−0.0829***
	(0.010)	(0.012)	(0.013)	(0.013)	(0.022)	(0.017)
China	0.1578***	0.0883***	0.0799***	0.2071***	0.3974***	0.1113***
	(0.009)	(0.010)	(0.011)	(0.011)	(0.020)	(0.017)
Japan	−0.1419***	−0.0841***	−0.1485***	−0.1158***	−0.0710**	−0.3320***
	(0.012)	(0.016)	(0.015)	(0.016)	(0.029)	(0.024)
Russia	0.0118	0.0737***	0.0324**	0.0228*	−0.0406	−0.1186***
	(0.010)	(0.012)	(0.017)	(0.013)	(0.030)	(0.022)
South Africa	0.0618***	0.0562***	0.0257**	0.0837***	0.0708***	0.0538***
	(0.009)	(0.010)	(0.011)	(0.012)	(0.024)	(0.018)

(Continued)

Clusters

	(1)	(2)	(3)	(4)	(5)	(6)
	Overall approval	Government campaigns	Information nudges	Default rules	Subliminal ads	Other mandates
South Korea	0.0403***	0.0343***	0.0567***	0.0570***	0.1989***	-0.1050***
	(0.010)	(0.011)	(0.011)	(0.012)	(0.021)	(0.017)
Denmark	-0.1829***	-0.1703***	-0.2395***	-0.1466***	-0.2597***	-0.1875***
	(0.009)	(0.011)	(0.012)	(0.012)	(0.021)	(0.016)
France	-0.0385***	-0.0401***	-0.0162	-0.0644***	-0.1089***	0.0434***
	(0.009)	(0.011)	(0.012)	(0.012)	(0.023)	(0.016)
Germany	-0.0709***	-0.0652***	-0.0712***	-0.0879***	-0.1042***	-0.0109
	(0.009)	(0.011)	(0.012)	(0.012)	(0.022)	(0.016)
Hungary	-0.1488***	-0.1819***	-0.1685***	-0.1077***	-0.1470***	-0.1941***
	(0.011)	(0.013)	(0.014)	(0.013)	(0.023)	(0.017)
Italy	0.0105	0.0015	-0.0246**	0.0337***	0.0382	-0.0072
	(0.010)	(0.012)	(0.013)	(0.013)	(0.023)	(0.017)
United Kingdom	-0.0217**	-0.0350***	0.0101	-0.0398***	-0.0445**	0.0165
	(0.009)	(0.010)	(0.011)	(0.011)	(0.021)	(0.015)
USA	-0.0847***	-0.0625***	-0.1090***	-0.0524***	-0.1494***	-0.1464***
	(0.012)	(0.014)	(0.016)	(0.015)	(0.026)	(0.021)
2015/2016	0.0000	0.0000	0.0000	0.0000	0.0000	0.0000
	(.)	(.)	(.)	(.)	(.)	(.)
2017/2018	-0.0142**	-0.0250***	-0.0070	-0.0027	-0.0042	-0.0479***
	(0.006)	(0.008)	(0.008)	(0.008)	(0.013)	(0.011)
_cons	0.7333***	0.8129***	0.8429***	0.6870***	0.6287***	0.6402***
	(0.009)	(0.010)	(0.012)	(0.011)	(0.021)	(0.016)
N	20,501	20,501	20,501	20,501	20,501	20,501
Adj. R2	0.148	0.087	0.089	0.116	0.089	0.088

Notes: "_cons" means the regression "constant" (intercept). It shows the value of the intercept of the model. "Adj. R2" means "adjusted R^2", a measure for the goodness of fit of the model. Values closer to 1 indicate a better fit.

7

EDUCATIVE NUDGES AND NONEDUCATIVE NUDGES

In terms of law and public policy, it is useful to distinguish between educative and noneducative nudges. Educative nudges include disclosure requirements, reminders, and warnings, which are specifically designed to increase people's own powers of agency. Noneducative nudges include default rules and uses of order effects (as on a menu or at a cafeteria), which are designed to preserve freedom of choice, but without necessarily increasing individual agency.

Our principal question here is whether people prefer educative nudges. As we will see, the answer is complicated. The simplest version is: They do. A more accurate and slightly more complex version is: They do, unless they are told that noneducative nudges are more effective. But the full story is far more interesting.

Two systems

Within behavioral science, some people have found it helpful to distinguish between two families of cognitive operations in the human mind: System 1, which is fast, automatic, and intuitive; and System 2, which is slow, calculative, and deliberative.[1] When people recognize a smiling face,

---

1 See Daniel Kahneman, *Thinking, Fast and Slow* (2011). The idea of two systems is controversial, and it is reasonable to ask what, exactly, the idea is meant to capture. For

add three plus three, or know how to get to their bathroom in the middle of the night, System 1 is at work. When people first learn to drive, when they multiply 563 times 322, or when they choose a medical plan among several hard-to-distinguish alternatives, they must rely on System 2.

System 1 can and often does get things right. As Daniel Kahneman and Shane Frederick write, "Although System 1 is more primitive than System 2, it is not necessarily less capable."[2] Through fast and frugal heuristics, people can perform exceedingly well. Any professional athlete has an educated System 1; Serena Williams knows what shot to hit in an instant. As a result of years of practice, an experienced lawyer, judge, doctor, or engineer has a well-trained System 1, and trained intuitions are often on the mark. At the same time, System 2 is hardly unerring. On multiplication problems, or in choosing among health care plans, people often make mistakes, even if they are trying very hard.[3]

Nonetheless, System 1 is distinctly associated with identifiable behavioral biases, producing a wide range of problems for policy and law. People sometimes show "present bias," focusing on the short term and downplaying the future. Most people tend to be unrealistically optimistic.[4] People use heuristics, or mental shortcuts, that usually work well, but that sometimes lead them in unfortunate directions. With respect to probability, people's intuitions may go badly wrong, in the sense that they produce serious mistakes, including life-altering ones.[5] To be sure, our intuitions are both adequate and helpful in the situations in which we ordinarily find ourselves. But there is no question that intuitions can badly misfire, and that a good nudge, and good choice architecture, will often provide indispensable help.

Educative nudges, offered by government agencies, attempt to strengthen the hand of System 2 by improving the role of deliberation and people's

---

example, something very different from a two-system account is offered in E. A. Phelps et al., Emotion and Decision Making: Multiple Modulatory Neural Circuits, *Ann. Rev of Neuroscience* 263, 37 (2014). Following Kahneman, we understand the idea as a useful fiction, not referring to "systems in the standard sense of entities with interacting aspects or parts." Kahneman, *supra* note, at 29. For those who reject the terminology, or are skeptical of it, it might be helpful simply to distinguish between noneducative and educative nudges, and to see the survey here as asking when people prefer one or another.

2 Daniel Kahneman and Shane Frederick, Representativeness Revisited: Attribute Substitution in Intuitive Judgment, in *Heuristics and Biases: The Psychology of Intuitive Judgement* 49, 51 (Thomas Gilovich et al., eds., 2002).

3 See Eric Johnson et al., Can Consumers Make Affordable Care Affordable? The Value of Choice Architecture, *PLOS One* 8, 1 (2013).

4 See Tali Sharot, *The Optimistic Bias* (2011).

5 For a powerful demonstration, see Daniel L. Chen et al., Decision-Making under the Gambler's Fallacy: Evidence from Asylum Judges, Loan Officers, and Baseball Umpires, *The Quarterly J. Econ.* 131, 1181 (2016).

considered judgments. The most obvious example is disclosure of relevant information. Some kinds of nudges, sometimes described as "boosts,"[6] attempt to improve people's capacity to make choices for themselves, for example by improving statistical literacy.

Noneducative nudges are designed to appeal to, or to activate, System 1. Graphic health warnings can be seen as an example, at least if they are not understood as having the purpose or effect of education. We might distinguish between System 2 disclosures, designed simply to give people factual information and to ask them to process it, and System 1 disclosures, designed to work on the automatic system (for example, by inculcating fear or hope). Some nudges do not appeal to System 1, strictly speaking, but turn out to work because of its operation—as, for example, where default rules have large effects in part because of the power of inertia, or where the ordering of items on some kind of menu affects what people choose, because of the selective nature of attention.[7] Nudges of this kind can be seen as "exploiting" the operations of System 1, though it would be more neutral to say that they take account of those operations, acknowledging that some form of choice architecture, affecting System 1, may be inevitable.

As we understand them here, System 2 nudges are specifically designed to increase people's capacity to exercise their own agency. On ethical and other grounds, they might seem better for that reason. Thus Jeremy Waldron writes: "I wish, though, that I could be made a better chooser rather than having someone on high take advantage (even for my own benefit) of my current thoughtlessness and my shabby intuitions."[8]

In the abstract, that is an honorable wish. As a matter of principle, the challenge arises when it is costly and difficult to make people better choosers—and when the net benefits of a System 1 nudge are far higher than the net benefits of a System 2 nudge. System 1 nudges, such as automatic enrollment, make life much simpler, and that is no small gain. There is also evidence that System 2 nudges can affect beliefs without affecting behavior, and that System 1 nudges can be more effective in altering what people actually do. The choice between System 1 nudges and System 2 nudges raises pervasive and fundamental questions about agency, freedom, and welfare.

---

6 Ralph Hertwig, When to Consider Boosting: Some Rules for Policymakers, *Behavioural Public Policy* 1, 143 (2017).

7 Eran Dayan and Maya Bar-Hillel, Nudge to Nobesity II: Menu Positions Influence Food Orders, *Judgement and Decision Making* 6, 333 (2011); Daniel R. Feenberg et al., *It's Good to be First: Order Bias in Reading and Citing*, NBER Working Papers (Working Paper No. 21141) (2015), available at www.nber.org/papers/w21141.

8 See Jeremy Waldron, It's All For Your Own Good, *NY Rev of Books* (2014), available at www.nybooks.com/articles/archives/2014/oct/09/cass-sunstein-its-all-your-own-good/.

The project here

Our major goal here is to report the results of a nationally representative survey in the United States, designed to elicit people's preferences between System 1 nudges and System 2 nudges in diverse contexts. We emphasize that our study is limited to Americans.[9] Administered by Survey Sampling International, the survey included more than 2,800 people, who were paid for their participation.

In brief, seven different groups, each consisting of more than 400 people, were asked to register their preferences with respect to different pairs of nudges. Four of those pairs involved areas in which nudges have often been used as policy tools: savings, smoking, clean energy, and water conservation.[10] In many ways, these pairs can be seen as standard, illustrating, as they do, dilemmas that can be found in multiple domains. Three of the pairs involved areas that raise highly distinctive issues and concerns: voter registration, childhood obesity, and abortion.

With respect to the four initial issues, the first finding is that in a neutral condition, in which participants receive no information about effectiveness, majorities prefer System 2 nudges. Notably, Americans are also divided, with between 26 percent and 45 percent favoring System 1 nudges. In the neutral condition, two of the four issues produce no significant differences among Democrats, Republicans, and independents. And while two of the issues did produce such differences, with a higher percentage of Democrats favoring System 1 nudges, the differences are relatively small.

The second finding is that when people are asked to assume that the System 1 nudge is "significantly more effective," many of them shift in its direction—but the shift is relatively modest, usually in the vicinity of

---

9 Several other studies, with different designs, have explored this question. *See* Gidon Felsen et al., Decisional Enhancement and Autonomy: Public Attitudes Toward Overt and Covert Nudges, *Judgement and Decision Making* 8, 203 (2012) (testing people's attitude toward employment prospects, and finding generally high levels of approval of System 2 nudges); Janice Jung and Barbara Mellers, American Attitudes Toward Nudges, *Judgement and Decision Making* 11, 62 (2016) (finding that on bounded scales, people generally prefer System 2 nudges); Ayala Arad and Ariel Rubinstein, The People's Perspective on Libertarian Paternalistic Policies, *J. Law and Economics* 61(2), 311–333 (2018) (finding evidence of "reactance" against System 1 nudges and some inclination to prefer System 2 nudges). The findings here are broadly compatible with those in these earlier papers.

10 We borrow the water conservation example from Janice Jung and Barbara Mellers, American Attitudes Toward Nudges, *Judgement and Decision Making* 11, 62 (2016).

about 12 percentage points. The third finding is that when people are asked to assume specific numbers, offering a quantitative demonstration that System 1 nudges are more effective, the shift in their direction is essentially the same in magnitude. The fourth and final finding is that when people are asked to assume that System 2 nudges are "significantly more effective," there is no shift in the direction of those nudges. This is an especially surprising finding, and we will attempt to explain it.

The most obvious interpretation of these findings is that in important contexts, most people want to protect and promote people's agency, and so they will favor System 2 nudges—but they also care about effectiveness, and so will turn to System 1 nudges if the evidence shows that they are significantly better. At the same time, there is significant heterogeneity within the American population. Many people prefer System 1 nudges, perhaps on the ground that they are more effective, perhaps on the ground that they make life simpler and easier. Some people appear not to have any abstract preference between System 1 nudges and System 2 nudges; apparently they care only about effectiveness.

By contrast, some people have a strong preference for the latter, and will require compelling evidence of superior effectiveness in order to favor System 1 nudges. Because significant numbers of Americans show no inclination to prefer System 1 nudges even when asked to assume that they are clearly more effective, we can safely say that some segment of the population would demand very powerful evidence to favor System 1 nudges—and perhaps no evidence would be sufficient.

With respect to voter registration, childhood obesity, and abortion, the patterns are illuminatingly different. For the first two, majorities do not favor System 2 nudges. On the contrary, automatic voter registration has clear majority support, and for childhood obesity, cafeteria design is preferred to parental education. Asking people to assume the significantly greater effectiveness of the System 1 nudge does increase the level of support, but it is high even without that information. The best explanations for the preference for System 1 nudges involve people's judgments about protection of the franchise (arguing in favor of automatic registration) and protection of children (favoring cafeteria design).

With respect to reducing the number of abortions, majorities consistently favor System 2 nudges, and that preference does not shift when people are asked to assume that System 1 nudges are more effective—undoubtedly because of a belief, on the part of many, that it is not appropriate for public officials to appeal to System 1 to discourage women from making their own choices. Notably, Republicans, Democrats, and independents all favor System 2 nudges in the abortion setting, though in most conditions, the level of support for System 1 nudges is significantly lower among Democrats. The sharp distinction between majority approval of a System 1 nudge for voting and majority approval of a System 2 nudge for abortion attests to the importance of people's judgments about whether a right is at stake—and whether a nudge is promoting or undermining it.

These findings support a variety of conclusions. In significant domains, majorities will prefer System 2 nudges to System 1 nudges, but there is likely to be real division on that issue. If System 1 nudges are shown to be more effective, there will be a shift in their direction, but it will not be as dramatic as might be anticipated, apparently because some people put a high premium on personal agency. Insofar as children are involved, System 1 nudges will be more welcome, and the same is true if System 1 nudges facilitate people's ability to enjoy something that qualifies as a right. If, on the other hand, any kind of nudge is compromising what people regard as a right, it will be rejected, and a System 2 nudge will be preferred, because it shows greater respect for individual agency.

In important respects, the survey findings are consistent with what emerges from a more sustained analysis of the normative issues; we sketch the central ingredients of that analysis here. Both the findings and the analysis bear on a variety of issues in law and policy. They suggest reasons to prefer System 2 nudges, such as disclosure of statistical information or some kind of education, but they also suggest that in many contexts, System 1 nudges, such as default rules, are preferable. System 1 might be inclined to favor System 2 nudges, and System 2 will frequently concur, but for many rights and interests, System 2 will ultimately decide that System 1 nudges are best.

Savings, smoking, and the environment

The first four questions asked people to choose among some familiar interventions, in areas that are familiar in law and policy.[11] Here are the four pairs:

11 See, e.g., Christine Jolls, Product Warnings, Debiasing, and Free Speech: The Case of Tobacco Regulation, J. Institutional and Theoretical Econ. 53, 169 (2013); Raj Chetty et al., Active vs. Passive Decisions and Crowd out in Retirement Savings Accounts: Evidence from Denmark (Working Paper No. 18565) (2012), www.nber.org/papers/w18565; Felix Ebeling and Sebastian Lotz, Domestic Uptake of Green Energy Promoted by Opt-Out Tariffs, Nature Climate Change 5, 868 (2015).

Which of these policies do you prefer, as part of an antismoking campaign?

1) Graphic warnings, with vivid pictures of people who are sick from cancer.

2) Purely factual information, giving people statistical information about the risks from smoking.

Which of these policies do you prefer, as part of a campaign to encourage people to save for retirement?

1) Automatic enrollment of employees in savings plans, subject to "opt out" if employees do not want to participate.

2) Financial literacy programs at the workplace, so that employees are educated about retirement options.

Which of these policies do you prefer, as part of a program to reduce pollution?

1) Automatic enrollment of customers in slightly more expensive "green" (environmentally friendly) energy, subject to "opt out" if customers want another, slightly less expensive energy source.

2) Educational campaigns so that consumers can learn the advantages of green (environmentally friendly) energy.

Which of these policies do you prefer, as a way of encouraging water conservation?

1) The government requires hotels to select a default policy of "environment-friendly rooms" in which towels left on the racks are not washed. If people want their towels washed, they can tell the front desk, and their towels will be washed daily.

2) The government requires hotels to provide guests with information about an "environment-friendly" policy in which towels left on the racks are not washed. People are encouraged to choose to take part, but if they do not choose to do so, their towels will be washed every day.

Neutral condition

In a neutral condition, in which people were provided with no information about effectiveness, majorities consistently showed a clear preference for System 2 nudges. The aggregate data is presented in Table 7.1.

It should be noted that the preference for System 2 nudges is strongest in the cases of green energy and water conservation. With respect to green energy, the likely theory is that it is better for people to learn, and to make

Table 7.1 Support for System 1 and System 2 nudges

	Percentage of respondents (N=430) who:	
Question	Prefer System 1 nudge	Prefer System 2 nudge
Smoking	45%	55%
Saving	43%	57%
Energy	26%	74%
Water	32%	68%

their own choices, than for them to be defaulted into an energy source that might turn out to be more expensive or less reliable. Participants might well have been concerned that people would not take the trouble to opt out and might thus have faced higher electricity bills without their explicit consent. In the case of water conservation, money is not involved, but more people also favored System 2 nudges, perhaps because of a concern about defaulting guests into a situation that might not be in their interest (involving unwashed and perhaps dirty towels).

It should also be noted that while the preference for System 2 nudges is consistent, large numbers of people favor System 1 nudges in all four contexts. One reason might be that they believe them to be more effective, so long as no information is provided on that question. The 45 percent level of support for graphic warnings for cigarettes might well have been based on a judgment that if the goal is to address a serious public health problem, such warnings are better than purely factual information. Another reason might be that some System 1 nudges might seem to impose lower decision-making burdens on choosers, as in the cases of default rules for saving, energy, and water conservation. If a System 1 nudge makes things easier for people, and does not require them to act, it might appear to be preferable.

System 1 nudges "significantly more effective"

In the neutral condition, people's preferences could have any number of sources. To obtain some understanding of what motivated those preferences, a different group of people was asked to assume that the System 1 nudge was "significantly more effective." The hypothesis was that these three words would lead to a major shift in the direction of System 1 nudges. The hypothesis was confirmed, but in a qualified way (see Table 7.2).

There are two noteworthy results here. First, the shift in the direction of System 1 nudges is significant for all four issues (using chi-square analysis,

Table 7.2 Preference when System 1 nudge "significantly more effective"

	Percentage of respondents who prefer System 1 nudge	
Question	Neutral condition (N = 430)	Told that System 1 nudge is "significantly more effective" (N = 407)
Smoking	45%	57%
Saving	43%	55%
Energy	26%	38%
Water	32%	42%

two-tailed p < 0.05 for each question); but it is not massive. Second, the shift is essentially the same for all four questions. Indeed, it is remarkably consistent, with no significant differences across questions. Informed of the greater effectiveness of System 1 nudges, there is a general movement of 10 to 12 percentage points.

We do not have enough data to speak of anything like an iron law here, but it is not too speculative to say that many Americans think that System 2 nudges will be more effective or instead believe that System 2 nudges are a better way of respecting people's agency—but they will shift when they receive information about the comparative effectiveness of System 1 nudges. At the same time, many people (usually 40 percent or more) will have a strong commitment, visceral or otherwise, to the superiority of the System 2 nudge. The addition of three words ("significantly more effective") will not change that commitment.

Numbers

The words "significantly more effective" have a high degree of opacity. It is not clear what they mean. Once they are specified in quantitative terms, they might have a stronger or weaker impact. Suppose, for example, that people were told to assume that automatic enrollment would increase participation in savings plans from 40 percent to 90 percent, or that graphic warnings would save 200,000 lives annually—but that the System 2 alternatives would have essentially no impact. Under those assumptions, it would not be easy to reject the idea that System 1 nudges are better. To reject that idea, one would have to have concerns about the outcomes (saving lives is good, but increased participation in savings plans is less obvious), or to put a very high premium indeed on a certain conception of personal agency.

To understand the effects of quantitative information, participants were asked to assume specified numerical disparities in favor of System

1 nudges—not as stark as in the examples just given, but nonetheless lopsided.

- **Smoking**: "Assume that [the System 1 nudge] is far more effective. It reduces smoking by 20 percent, while [the System 2 nudge] reduces smoking by 5 percent."
- **Saving**: "Assume that [the System 1 nudge] is far more effective. It leads 90 percent of workers to enroll in savings plans, whereas [the System 2 nudge] leads only 55 percent to enroll in such plans."
- **Energy**: "Assume that [the System 1 nudge] is far more effective. It cuts pollution by 40 percent, whereas [the System 2 nudge] cuts pollution by just 5 percent."
- **Water**: "Assume that [the System 1 nudge] is far more effective. On average it cuts water use from washing towels by 70 percent, whereas [the System 2 nudge] cuts water use from washing towels by 10 percent."

The results are illustrated in Table 7.3.

It should be clear that the quantitative information did not have a larger effect than the words "significantly more effective." Quite surprisingly, that information produced no statistically significant changes. One reason may be that the numerical differences were not so extreme; they plausibly reflected the kind of disparity that a purely qualitative account ("significantly more effective") would suggest. If so, the numbers provided no additional information. Another reason may be that the people who favored System 2 nudges, even in the face of a qualitative explanation that it would be less effective, did so because of a strong preference for what they saw as personal agency, and hence could not be moved even by fairly impressive numbers.

Table 7.3 Preference for System 1 nudges with quantitative information

Question	Percentage of respondents who prefer System 1 nudge		
	Neutral condition (N = 430)	Told that System 1 nudge is "significantly more effective" (N = 407)	Told that System 1 nudge is more effective, with quantification (N = 435)
Smoking	45%	57%	58%
Saving	43%	55%	56%
Energy	26%	38%	43%
Water	32%	42%	47%

System 2 nudges "significantly more effective"

If it is assumed that System 2 nudges are "significantly more effective," we might expect that very large majorities would endorse them. If a nudge increases people's own capacities and also produces the desired result, it would seem far preferable to a less effective intervention that does not educate people in any way. The principal qualification is that if a nudge is effective in producing a result that people do not like, then they will of course reject it for that very reason. (Most people would not like a nudge that is effective in encouraging people to use illegal drugs or to text while driving.) We will return to this point. The results are presented in Table 7.4.

Most surprisingly, the assumption of the comparatively greater effectiveness of System 2 nudges does not produce any shift in their direction. The numbers are essentially identical—a highly unexpected finding. Any explanation remains speculative, but it is possible that those who supported System 2 nudges already assumed that they would be more effective, so that the three additional words added no new information.

Alternatively, some people might think that System 1 nudges have some independent advantage, or that System 2 nudges have some independent disadvantage. System 1 supporters might have stronger preference than System 2 supporters and thus are less likely to be persuaded by effectiveness arguments. Automatic enrollment in a savings plan might be more desirable than financial literacy programs, simply because they do not impose the costs and burdens of the latter. The same is true of automatic enrollment in green energy. It is also true that most people already prefer System 2 nudges and hence fewer people are available to be moved.

If so, then the lack of an effect from the System-2-nudge-is-more-effective assumption is similar to the lack of effect of quantitative

Table 7.4 Preference for System 1 nudges when System 2 nudge is "significantly more effective"

	Percentage of respondents who prefer System 1 nudge	
Question	Neutral condition	Told that System 2 nudge is "significantly more effective"
Smoking	45%	43%
Saving	43%	44%
Energy	26%	26%
Water	32%	29%

information. Some people prefer System 1 nudges even if they believe them to be less effective. They might be engaged in some kind of informal cost–benefit analysis—a point to which we will return.

Political divisions

Do political affiliations explain people's preferences for System 1 or System 2 nudges? The results are presented in full in Tables 7.5, 7.6, 7.7, 7.8.

There are many numbers here, but the basic story is straightforward. Republicans, Democrats, and independents all favor System 2 nudges, with just one qualification: Democrats are evenly split with respect to anti-smoking nudges. Both qualitative and quantitative information about the greater effectiveness of System 1 nudges produces an increase of about 10 to 20 percent in favor of System 1 nudges—and essentially the same degree of change is observed for all three groups. For all three groups, assuming that System 2 nudges are

Table 7.5 Support for System 1 and System 2 nudges by partisan affiliation

CONDITION 1	Percentage of respondents[12] who:					
Question	Prefer System 1 nudge			Prefer System 2 nudge		
	Dem.	Rep.	Indep.	Dem.	Rep.	Indep.
Smoking	50%	44%	40%	50%	56%	60%
Saving	42%	48%	39%	58%	52%	61%
Energy	34%	24%	19%	66%	76%	81%
Water	42%	27%	26%	58%	73%	74%

Table 7.6 Preference when System 1 nudge "significantly more effective" by partisan affiliation

CONDITION 2	Percentage of respondents[13] who:					
Question	Prefer System 1 nudge			Prefer System 2 nudge		
	Dem.	Rep.	Indep.	Dem.	Rep.	Indep.
Smoking	62%	57%	52%	38%	43%	48%
Saving	60%	55%	49%	40%	45%	51%
Energy	48%	31%	34%	52%	69%	66%
Water	51%	36%	38%	49%	64%	62%

12 163 Democrats; 142 Republicans; 125 independents.
13 163 Democrats; 142 Republicans; 125 independents.

Table 7.7 Preference with quantitative information by partisan affiliation

CONDITION 3	Percentage of respondents[14] who:					
Question	Prefer System 1 nudge			Prefer System 2 nudge		
	Dem.	Rep.	Indep.	Dem.	Rep.	Indep.
Smoking	61%	56%	56%	39%	44%	44%
Saving	58%	51%	57%	42%	49%	43%
Energy	47%	38%	42%	53%	62%	58%
Water	52%	41%	48%	48%	59%	52%

Table 7.8 Preference when System 2 nudge is "significantly more effective" by partisan affiliation

CONDITION 4	Percentage of respondents[15] who:					
Question	Prefer System 1 nudge			Prefer System 2 nudge		
	Dem.	Rep.	Indep.	Dem.	Rep.	Indep.
Smoking	53%	35%	39%	47%	65%	61%
Saving	47%	37%	47%	53%	63%	53%
Energy	28%	24%	25%	72%	76%	75%
Water	41%	20%	23%	59%	80%	77%

significantly more effective produces results quite similar to those in the neutral condition. Perhaps most remarkably: None of the differences between condition 1 and condition 4, for any partisan affiliation, is statistically significant.

The largest and most important finding here is that in a majority of the conditions, the differences among Democrats, Republicans, and independents are not significant. Their judgments, as between System 1 and System 2 nudges, are broadly in line with one another. But in some conditions, Democrats are more inclined to System 1 nudges than are Republicans and independents. In all conditions, for example, Democrats are more favorably disposed than Republicans or independents to a System 1 nudge for water conservation; the difference is significant (p <0.05). In condition 2, Democrats are more favorably disposed than Republicans or independents to a System 1 nudge for energy. In condition 4, Democrats are more favorably disposed than Republicans to a System 1 nudge for smoking.

14 165 Democrats; 138 Republicans; 132 independents.
15 169 Democrats; 131 Republicans; 133 independents.

We can offer some plausible explanations for these differences. Democrats are comparatively more enthusiastic about green energy and water conservation, and very possibly anti-smoking efforts as well; to them, a System 1 nudge might seem more appealing if it is thought to be more effective. Republicans might be more likely to favor a System 2 nudge, especially for green energy or water conservation, in order to preserve personal agency. Notably, however, there are no significant differences among the three groups in terms of movements across conditions.

Voting, children, and abortion

The range of System 1 and System 2 nudges is of course exceptionally wide. For example, some nudges promote rights, by making them easier to enjoy; consider, for example, simplified voter registration. Some nudges involve children. Teachers impose mandates on elementary school children, but they also nudge them, in various ways, to do their homework, to act courteously, and to avoid disrupting classes. Some nudges discourage the use of rights. We could easily imagine efforts to steer people away from certain religious practices, or to discourage them from exercising their right to sexual privacy; pro-abstinence nudges are an example.

As illustrations of these distinctive kinds of nudges, we tested people's judgments about voting, childhood obesity, and abortion. The three pairs looked like this:

Which of these policies do you prefer, as part of a program to increase voter registration?

1) Automatic voter registration, so that when people receive their driver's licenses, and show they are domiciled in your state, they are automatically registered as voters.

2) A public education campaign to convince people to register to vote.

Which of these policies do you prefer, as part of a program to combat childhood obesity?

1) Redesigning school cafeterias so that healthy, low-calorie options are in the most visible locations.

2) Educating parents about the problem of childhood obesity and how to combat it.

Which of these policies do you prefer, as a means of discouraging abortions? (Please indicate which you prefer even if you do not like either.)

1) Requiring pregnant women, before having an abortion, to see vivid photos of fetuses, designed to show that they are merely very young children.

2) Requiring pregnant women, before having an abortion, to speak briefly with a doctor about whether they really believe, on reflection, that an abortion is the right choice, in light of the moral issues involved.

General results

Most Americans prefer automatic voter registration to efforts to encourage people to register. With the three variations, the changes in assumptions are not statistically significant (condition 1 is neutral; condition 2 assumes that System 1 nudge is significantly more effective; condition 3 assumes quantitative evidence of the superior effectiveness of System 1 nudges; condition 4 assumes that System 2 nudge is significantly more effective) (see Table 7.9).

There are two noteworthy findings here. The first is that a majority prefers the System 1 nudge. The reason is probably a judgment or intuition that people should be voters "by default"; they should not have to take steps to attain that status. The second is that with respect to automatic voter registration, movements do not occur across the three conditions, as they sometimes do for the four nudges previously discussed. In particular, we observe movements from condition 1 to conditions 2 and 3 for the four standard nudges; no such movements are found here.

For childhood obesity, a small majority favors cafeteria design over parental education, except when people are asked to assume that the latter is significantly more effective, as is shown in Table 7.10.

Table 7.9 Voter registration

Voter registration	Percentage of respondents who:	
Condition	Prefer System 1 nudge	Prefer System 2 nudge
1	57%	43%
2	62%	38%
3	61%	39%
4	52%	48%

Table 7.10 Childhood obesity

Childhood obesity	Percentage of respondents who:	
Condition	Prefer System 1 nudge	Prefer System 2 nudge
1	53%	47%
2	53%	47%
3	63%	37%
4	48%	52%

Table 7.11 Abortion

Abortion	Percentage of respondents who:	
Condition	Prefer System 1 nudge	Prefer System 2 nudge
1	25%	75%
2	34%	66%
3	33%	67%
4	29%	71%

In the three "informed" conditions, only one shift is significant: With quantitative information, there is an increase in support for cafeteria design. In general, we do not find the same kinds of shifts as are observed for the four more standard nudges.

For abortion, the System 2 nudge is preferred by a substantial majority. (Note that for this question, it was specifically requested that participants chose one even if they do not like either, acknowledging that on that highly sensitive issue, some respondents might reject both nudges.) The preference for the System 2 nudge does not shift significantly across the four conditions (see Table 7.11).

Political divisions

What is the role of political divisions? We might well expect that it would be larger than in the four standard cases, and in some respects it is, but the full story is not entirely straightforward, the results for which are in Tables 7.12, 7.13, and 7.14.

The most consistent difference can be found in the area of abortion, where higher percentages of Republicans are more inclined to favor the

Table 7.12 Voter registration by partisan affiliation

| Voter registration—by party | Percentage of respondents who: | | | | | |
| Condition | Prefer System 1 nudge | | | Prefer System 2 nudge | | |
	Dem.	Rep.	Indep.	Dem.	Rep.	Indep.
1	65%	53%	52%	35%	47%	43%
2	63%	53%	57%	37%	47%	43%
3	71%	54%	58%	29%	46%	42%
4	55%	53%	48%	45%	47%	52%

Table 7.13 Childhood obesity by partisan affiliation

| Childhood obesity—by party | Percentage of respondents who: | | | | | |
| Condition | Prefer System 1 nudge | | | Prefer System 2 nudge | | |
	Dem.	Rep.	Indep.	Dem.	Rep.	Indep.
1	61%	45%	51%	39%	54%	49%
2	59%	48%	52%	41%	52%	48%
3	70%	52%	67%	30%	48%	33%
4	51%	43%	49%	49%	57%	51%

Table 7.14 Abortion by partisan affiliation

| Abortion—by party | Percentage of respondents who: | | | | | |
| Condition | Prefer System 1 nudge | | | Prefer System 2 nudge | | |
	Dem.	Rep.	Indep.	Dem.	Rep.	Indep.
1	20%	32%	23%	80%	68%	77%
2	30%	42%	29%	70%	58%	71%
3	25%	43%	31%	75%	57%	69%
4	24%	34%	30%	76%	66%	70%

System 1 nudge. In three of the four conditions, the difference for that question is statistically significant[16] between Democrats and Republicans (condition 4 is the exception). For both voting and childhood obesity, the difference between Democrats and Republicans is significant for

16 Using chi-square analysis, two-tailed $p < 0.05$ for each question.

conditions 1 and 3. Democrats and independents show a significant difference for voting in conditions 1 and 3. Republicans and independents show such a difference for abortion in conditions 2 and 3; Republicans and independents show such a difference for childhood obesity in condition 3. Interestingly, there is no significant difference of any kind in condition 4.

Here as well, the details should not obscure the basic story. For the four standard cases, political affiliation usually did not explain people's choices between System 1 and System 2 nudges (with interesting exceptions, especially in the case of green energy). Political affiliation mattered more for abortion, voting, and childhood obesity. It would not, of course, be surprising to find that Democrats are less supportive of pro-life nudges than are Republicans, or that Republicans are less enthusiastic than Democrats about automatic voter registration or efforts to combat childhood obesity (see Chapter 2). The point is that in politically contested issues, there is a partisan difference in terms of choice between System 1 and System 2 nudges. Apparently it is the case that if people strongly support a particular end, they will be more likely to support a System 1 nudge to attain it.

Within-subjects

The foregoing findings involved a "between subjects" design. Different groups of participants saw different conditions, rather than all of them at once. That design has significant advantages, because it prevents contamination by previous answers. If questions are seen in isolation, responses cannot be affected by order effects, or by a particular factor that becomes highlighted only by virtue of its clear difference from a previous question.

Nonetheless, there are advantages to a "within-subjects" design, by which participants see, and answer, all of the questions in the same survey. The principal advantage is that with a within-subjects design, it is possible to test whether people's original answers shift after they are given information about comparative effectiveness. That question is important to test, because it reveals whether some people are strongly committed to System 1 or System 2 nudges—so committed that they will stick with one or the other even when effectiveness information stares them in the face.

To explore that issue, we used Amazon Mechanical Turk to ask about 400 people 24 questions, involving all of the areas tested above (with the exception of abortion[17]). Notably, this is not a random sample, and hence it would be hazardous to draw conclusions about the sources of differences between this group and the nationally representative one. With that caveat, the results are in Table 7.15.

Several things are relatively clear. In general, the answers in the neutral condition are fairly close to what was found in the nationally representative sample. At the same time, and as expected, the movements across conditions are somewhat greater. In particular, we observe movements of at least 25 percent from condition 1 to condition 3 for four more standard questions. And for all questions, movements of at least 11 percent, and sometimes of more than 20 percent, can be found from condition 1 to condition 4. In this survey, the differences among the conditions produced larger shifts in people's views.

There are two important qualifications. First, at least one-third of the population continued to favor the System 2 nudge in the within-subjects condition, even when they were given numbers to support the comparatively greater effectiveness of the System 1 nudge. Second, large percentages of people (usually around one-quarter) continued to favor the System 1 nudge in the within-subjects condition, even when they were informed that the System 2 nudge was significantly more effective.

Although it does not involve a nationally representative sample, the within-subjects study provides useful information. It suggests that the number of

Table 7.15 Within-subjects results

	Percentage of respondents who prefer System 1 nudge			
Question	Neutral condition	Told that System 1 nudge is "significantly more effective"	Told that System 1 nudge is "significantly more effective," with quantification	Told that System 2 nudge is "significantly more effective"
Smoking	41%	57%	67%	30%
Saving	45%	58%	72%	28%
Energy	36%	50%	69%	19%
Water	42%	55%	67%	21%
Obesity	61%	71%	78%	29%
Voting	60%	66%	76%	34%

17 This area was excluded on the ground that it is highly controversial, and it is not clear how much more would be learned in a within-subjects design.

people who shift to System 1 nudges will probably be greater in a within-subjects design—and that the appeal of the System 2 nudge will be heightened, in that design, with evidence of greater effectiveness. At the same time, it fortifies the general conclusion that a certain percentage of the population will favor System 2 nudges even if they are significantly less effective, in large part because of a commitment to a certain conception of individual agency.

Popular opinion, law, and public policy

As we have emphasized, survey evidence can tell us a great deal about what kinds of policies will produce public approval or disapproval. We know that when people are not asked to choose between System 1 nudges and System 2 nudges, and are simply asked whether they approve of a nudge, they tend to favor both, including graphic warnings for smoking and distracted driving, and automatic enrollment in savings plans and green energy. We also know that Americans reject nudges that reflect what they see as illicit ends (such as religious favoritism) or that are inconsistent with the values and interests of most choosers (such as automatic contributions to particular charities). There is a concern about manipulation, at least in extreme cases, such as subliminal advertising to discourage smoking or use of visual illusions to encourage drivers to slow down.

We have also emphasized that the results of surveys may or may not track what would emerge from a sustained analysis. In fact we do not know exactly how people are thinking when they respond to survey questions. Consider an admittedly speculative hypothesis: *System 1 prefers System 2 nudges.* On this view, the automatic system favors System 2 nudges, and the deliberative system is necessary to override that form of favoritism. The data here are not sufficient to support that hypothesis; people's preference for System 1 nudges might be deliberative rather than automatic. But the hypothesis cannot be ruled out of bounds.

Consider another hypothesis: *System 2 favors System 1 nudges.* The data here are also insufficient to support that hypothesis, though it is imaginable that a careful analysis of various situations would suggest that System 1 nudges often or generally work better.

How should regulators think about the choice, having as they do a toolbox of instruments? It is possible, of course, that mandates will be better than nudges of any kind; perhaps they will be more effective and have higher net benefits. It is also possible that inaction is best, because any new intervention would have costs in excess of benefits. Economic incentives might be the best approach of all. But in many contexts, policymakers must specifically decide between System 1 nudges and System 2 nudges. To promote savings, they might engage in an educational campaign or opt for automatic enrollment; to promote access to public programs, they might rely on education or new default rules; to discourage smoking or distracted driving, they might rely on graphic warnings or a statistical presentation of some kind. How should they decide?

To come to terms with that question, it would be helpful to specify the foundations for any answer. Suppose that we are welfarists, believing that any evaluation has to turn on the effects of an intervention on social welfare.[18] If so, helpful questions are: What are the costs and what are the benefits of a System 1 or System 2 nudge? Which has higher net benefits? For these questions, information about effectiveness is relevant, but it is hardly sufficient. We need cost information as well. A maximally effective nudge might be too costly to be worthwhile, or it might have lower net benefits than a somewhat less effective but far less costly nudge.

In addition, the effectiveness information does not, by itself, give a full account of benefits. If 90 percent of people end up in savings plans, or if automatic enrollment in green energy cuts pollution by 20 percent, what exactly are the welfare consequences? Increases in participation rates and reductions in pollution seem desirable, but a great deal of further work would be needed to understand exactly how desirable they are. Are increases in participation rates important? How important? What are the mortality and morbidity consequences of cutting pollution levels by 20 percent? In this respect, the survey questions, even in the various conditions, failed to provide respondents with relevant information. It would be interesting, for example, to see how people's view would switch if they were asked to assume that for smoking, a System 1 nudge would prevent 4,000 more premature deaths than a System 2 nudge.

At first glance, welfarists would have no systematic reason to prefer System 1 nudges to System 2 nudges, or vice-versa. Everything turns on their costs and benefits.[19] But second-order considerations might cut in one or another

18 A welfarist approach is used in Ryan Bubb and Richard Pildes, How Behavioral Economics Trims Its Sails and Why, *Harv. L. Rev.* 127, 1593 (2014).

19 If a System 1 nudge causes a welfare loss because people resent it, that loss would of course have to be included. Cf. Sarah Conly, *Against Autonomy* (2012), at 156–59 (cataloguing welfare effects of soda regulation).

direction. Part of the welfare calculation involves the cost of nudging itself. Under imaginable conditions, System 1 nudges can be far simpler to implement (as, for example, when they involve a mere default rule). At the same time, it is relevant to ask about the long-term effects of a nudge. If a System 2 nudge would educate people, and have beneficial effects in multiple domains of their lives, then it would have ancillary benefits, and they might turn out to be significant. It is doubtful that survey responses are adequately capturing these points, though some respondents might be attentive to them.

Suppose that we are not welfarists and that we believe that for reasons that involve dignity or autonomy, people ought to be active agents, affirmatively responsible for outcomes that affect their lives. To be sure, this idea has considerable ambiguity, but something of this sort undergirds the judgment that even if automatic enrollment of some kind can promote people's welfare, it is more respectful to them, and therefore best for them, to become informed and then to choose.[20] Perhaps what is wrong with paternalism, even of the choice-preserving kind, is that it is insulting to people's capacity for agency; perhaps it shows a form of disrespect.[21] Why not educate people, rather than enrolling them in a program that government thinks is in their interest?

Different people who press this question might accept diverse kinds of answers. Some people might agree that if automatic enrollment is significantly better on welfare grounds, it is not necessary or preferable to educate people; but they would insist that the government must meet the burden of demonstrating that it is significantly better. Other people would adopt a strong presumption in favor of educative approaches and would demand an exceptionally strong demonstration of higher net benefits. Still others might believe that in at least some contests, no such demonstration could justify a System 1 nudge. A continuum of beliefs might well be imagined. Such a continuum would, of course, fit with the results here.

Agency

In some circles, there is a strong preference for interventions that augment people's capacities, and skepticism about forms of choice architecture that

---

20 Cf. Nicholas Cornell, A Third Theory of Paternalism, Mich. L. Rev. 113, 1295 (2015) (arguing that paternalism shows such disrespect).
21 Id. A powerful response can be found in Conly, *supra* note 105, arguing that it is not disrespectful for government to act on the basis of an accurate understanding of people's capacities.

seem to exploit or take advantage of people's fallibility. If a default rule works because of inertia, for example, it might be seen to be a form of manipulation, and even if that charge is far too strong, some people might contend that it is best to rely on education. On one view, the choice between System 1 and System 2 nudges depends on an assessment of comparative welfare effects, which requires a form of cost–benefit analysis.[22] On another view, concerns about autonomy and dignity deserve a central place.

Our major goal here has been to investigate what people actually think about these questions. A central finding is that most people usually do prefer System 2 nudges, at least in the class of cases that were tested. Moreover, the preference cuts across partisan lines. When participants are told to assume that System 1 nudges are more effective, many of them are in their direction—usually between 10 and 14 percent. When they are given quantitative information, specifying the greater effectiveness, the shift is essentially identical. And when people are asked to assume that System 2 nudges are significantly more effective, their judgments are about the same as in the neutral condition—a most unexpected finding.

Political differences emerge in several contexts. For example, Democrats are more inclined to favor System 1 nudges in the contexts of green energy and water conservation. But the more dramatic finding is that in general, Democrats, Republicans, and independents show strikingly similar patterns of responses. They tend to favor System 2 nudges, at least in the standard cases: to shift by the same percentages when they are asked to assume that the System 1 nudge is significantly more effective and that it has specified numerical advantages; and to show the same numbers as in the neutral condition when they are asked to assume that the System 2 nudge is significantly more effective.

As we have seen, different subject areas elicit different responses. If people care greatly about the end, perhaps effectiveness is all that matters, and the issue of agency will seem beside the point. For example, a System 1 nudge to reduce criminal violence might be preferred purely on effectiveness grounds, and people will not much care that a System 2 nudge preserves people's capacity to exercise their own agency (to murder or to rape). We can easily go further: If people are outraged by the conduct that is being targeted (murder, rape), and if they want to eliminate it, a man-

22 See Cass R. Sunstein, *The Cost–Benefit Revolution* (2018)

date will be entirely acceptable, and a System 1 nudge, complementing that mandate, will be unobjectionable in principle.

To the extent that the issue is polarizing on political grounds, we might also expect to see polarized judgments about which kind of nudge to favor. The abortion example is exemplary on that ground. We have seen that while most Democrats and most Republicans favor System 2 nudges to reduce abortions, the percentage of Republicans who favor System 1 nudges is significantly higher. For green energy and water conservation, there is a similar difference, but in the opposite direction. If people question or do not like the ends of those who deploy nudges, they might end up preferring System 2 nudges, because they seem better on autonomy grounds.

It should therefore be unsurprising that in some conditions we also find partisan differences with respect to voter registration and childhood obesity. These findings have large implications for judgments about nudging in general. They suggest that we will find comparative receptivity to System 1 nudges when the ends seem desirable and when people trust the officials who seek to secure them—and comparative skepticism about System 1 nudges when the ends seem questionable or the officials untrustworthy.

The most interesting question involves the precise tradeoff between sacrificing a degree of personal agency (as System 1 nudges might be taken to do) and increasing effectiveness. People put different weights on agency and understand it in different ways, and some of them will demand a steep price, in terms of effectiveness, in order to compromise it. Here as well, context matters, and so the value placed on agency will be high for some populations (with respect to, say, the abortion right), whereas it will be low for those very populations (with respect to, say, voter registration). The value of agency varies across persons and contexts.

Less obviously, and more intriguingly, the same is true for its sign. For some of the subjects of nudging, the exercise of agency is a cost rather than a benefit; voter registration is the most prominent case in point. A form of choice architecture that respects rights, and that does not require people to take action to enjoy them, might be strongly favored, simply on the ground that it makes things easy. The example suggests a larger point. System 1 might tend to prefer System 2 nudges, and System 2 might agree, but after sustained analysis, System 2 will often conclude that System 1 nudges are best.

8

MISCONCEPTIONS

Our principal goal here has been to present information about public opinion. We have only glanced at normative questions. But by way of clarification, we think that it will be useful to catalogue some common mistakes and misconceptions. Unfortunately, they continue to divert attention both in the public domain and in academic circles, and hence to stall progress. The good news is that survey evidence suggests that when people are asked concrete questions, they do not fall victim to these misconceptions. Abstractions appear to cause the trouble.

Without further ado:

1. *Nudges are an insult to human agency.*

In free societies, people are treated with respect. They are allowed to go their own way. Some people object that nudges are troublesome because they treat people as mere objects for official control.

The objection is off the mark. One of the main points of nudging is to preserve freedom of choice—and thus to maintain people's capacity for agency. Many nudges are self-consciously educative, and hence they strengthen that very capacity: consider calorie labels, or warnings about risks associated with certain products. With information, warnings, and reminders, people are in a better position to choose their own way. Noneducative nudges, such as uses of healthy choice architecture at cafeterias or in grocery stores, also allow people to choose as they wish. Survey evidence, suggesting widespread approval of both educative and noneducative nudges, testifies to general appreciation of these points.

Perhaps it could be argued that if the goal is to promote agency, default rules are problematic. But because such rules are omnipresent in human life, it is not easy to make that argument convincing. Would it make sense to excise default rules from the law of contract? To say that employers, hospitals, and banks are forbidden from using default rules? In practice, what would that even mean? Those who are inclined to reject default rules out of respect for individual agency would do well to ponder the countless contexts in which such rules make life simpler and easier to navigate. (On the immense importance of navigability, more in a moment.)

2. Nudges are based on excessive trust in government.

An intuitive objection to nudging is rooted in fear of government. To put that objection in its sharpest form: Suppose that public officials are incompetent, self-interested, reckless, or corrupt. Suppose that your least favorite leaders are or will be in charge. Would you want them to nudge? Or suppose that you are keenly alert to public choice problems, emphasized by James Buchanan and his followers, or "the knowledge problem," emphasized by Friedrich Hayek and his followers.[1] If interest groups are able to push government in their preferred directions, and if public officials lack crucial information, then you might insist: Do not nudge! Reliance on private markets might seem far better.

Indeed, behavioral science itself might be taken to put this conclusion in bold letters. There is no reason to think that public officials are immune to behavioral biases. In a democratic society, the electoral connection might mean that they will respond to the same biases that affect ordinary people. To be sure, structural safeguards might help, especially if they ensure a large place for technocrats, insistent on science and on careful attention to costs and benefits. But in any real-world polity, behavioral distortions are difficult to avoid.

These are fair and important points, but if they are taken as an objection to nudging, they run into a logical problem: a great deal of nudging is inevitable. So long as government has offices and websites, it will be nudging. If the law establishes contract, property, and tort law, it will be nudging, if only

---

1 Friedrich Hayek, The Use of Knowledge in Society, *Am. Econ. Rev.* 35, 519 (1945).

because it will set out default rules, which establish what happens if people do nothing. As Hayek himself wrote, the task of establishing a competitive system provides "indeed a wide and unquestioned field for state activity," for "in no system that could be rationally defended would the state just do nothing. An effective competitive system needs an intelligently designed and continuously adjusted legal framework as much as any other."[2]

As Hayek understood, a state that protects private property and that enforces contracts has to establish a set of prohibitions and permissions, including a set of default entitlements, establishing who has what before bargaining begins. For that reason, it is pointless to exclaim, "do not nudge!"—at least if one does not embrace anarchy.

The second answer to those who distrust government is that because nudges maintain freedom of choice, they offer a safety valve against official error. Those who favor nudges are keenly alert to the public choice problem and the knowledge problem, and to the possibility that public officials will show behavioral biases. Many of them are influenced by Buchanan and (especially) Hayek. If one distrusts government, the real focus should be on mandates, bans, subsidies, and taxes. To be sure, nudges ought not to be free from scrutiny, but they should be a relatively lower priority.

It is true, of course, that some nudging is optional. Government can warn people about smoking, opioid addiction, and distracted driving, or not. It can seek to protect consumers against deception and manipulation, or not. It can undertake public education campaigns, or not. If you think that government is entirely untrustworthy, you might want it to avoid nudging whenever it can.

In the abstract, that position cannot be ruled out of bounds. Public choice problems, and the knowledge problem, are real and important. On highly pessimistic assumptions about the capacities and incentives of public officials, and highly optimistic assumptions about the capacities and incentives of those in the private sector, nudging should be minimized. But private actors nudge, and sometimes it is very much in their interest to exploit cognitive biases, thus causing serious harm to countless people. Would it be a good idea to forbid public officials from taking steps to reduce smoking and distracted driving? In any case, the track record of real-world nudging includes impressive success stories, if success is measured by cost-effectiveness.[3]

2 Friedrich Hayek, *The Road to Serfdom* 88 (1943).
3 Shlomo Benartzi et al., Should Governments Invest More in Nudging?, *Psychol. Sci.* 28, 1041 (2017).

To be sure, nudges, like other interventions from such officials, should be constrained by democratic requirements, including transparency, public debate, and independent monitoring (including continuing evaluation of how they work in practice). Constraints of this kind can reduce the risks (without eliminating them). The fundamental point is that those risks are far larger with other tools, above all mandates and bans.

3. Nudges are covert.

Some people have argued that mandates, bans, and taxes have one advantage: They are transparent. People know what they are. No one is fooled. By contrast, nudges are covert and in that sense sneaky, a form of trickery.[4] They affect people without their knowledge.

For countless nudges, this objection is hard to understand. A GPS device nudges, and it is entirely transparent. Labels, warnings, and reminders are not exactly hidden; if they are, they will not work. When an employer automatically enrolls employees into a savings plan, subject to opt out, nothing is hidden. (If it is, there is a problem; the right to opt out should be clear.)

Why, then, have intelligent people objected that nudges are covert? Is there anything at all to that objection? One possibility is that when people participate in a randomized controlled trial, they may not be informed of that fact. (A randomized trial might not work if people are told about the various conditions.) But we suspect that the real answer is that some nudges work even though those who are affected by them do not focus on them, or even think about them. While such nudges are hardly hidden, people may be unaware of them, or at least unaware of their purposes and effects.

For example, a cafeteria might be designed so that the healthy foods are most visible and placed first, and people might choose them for that very reason. Such a design is not hidden—on the contrary, it should be obvious—but people may not be aware that their cafeteria has been designed so as to promote healthy choices. To be sure, they know that the fruits are more visible than the brownies, but they might not know why, and their decision to select a fruit might be quick and automatic rather than reflective. Or people might not think much about the default rules that come with (say) an agreement with a rental car company. If people are automatically enrolled into some kind of insurance plan and allowed to opt out, they might say, "yeah, whatever," and simply go along with the default.

4 Edward Glaeser, Paternalism and Policy, U. Chi. L. Rev. 73, 133 (2006).

In that sense, it is correct to say that some nudges can work even if or perhaps because people are unaware that they are being nudged. Note, however, that emerging evidence finds that the effects of such nudges are not diminished even if people are told that nudging is at work. Though research continues, transparency about the existence and justification of default rules appears not to reduce their impact in general.[5] For some people, such clarity may even increase that impact, by amplifying the informational signal that some default rules offer.[6] On plausible assumptions, drawing attention to the healthy design of a cafeteria will actually increase the effect of that design, because it will convey valuable information. (To be sure, it may produce "reactance" in some consumers.)

4. Nudges are manipulative.

In a variation on the claim that nudges are covert, some people have objected that nudges are a form of manipulation. But return to the points we have just explored: If people are reminded that they have a doctor's appointment next Thursday, no one is manipulating them. The same is true if people are given information about the caloric content of food or if they are warned that certain foods contain shellfish or nuts, or that if they take more than the recommended dosage of Benadryl, something bad might happen.

To be sure, most people reject subliminal advertising, apparently on the ground that it is manipulative. And we could imagine a graphic warning about opioid addiction, or about the use of cell phones while driving, that would create immediate fear or revulsion, or intensely engage people's emotions; it might be objected that nudges of this kind count as a form of manipulation. To know whether they do, we need a definition of manipulation. To make a (very) long and complex story short, philosophers and others have generally converged on the view that an action counts as manipulative if it bypasses people's capacity for rational deliberation.[7] On any view, most nudges do not qualify. True, some imaginable nudges might cross the line, but that is very different from saying that nudges are manipulative as such.

5 Hendrick Bruns et al., Can Nudges Be Transparent and Yet Effective?, Journal of Economic Psychology (2018); George Loewenstein, Warning: You Are About to be Nudged. Behavioral Sci. and Pol'y, 1, 35 (2015).

6 Craig McKenzie et al., Recommendations Implicit in Policy Defaults, Psychol. Sci. 17, 414 (2006).

7 Anne Barnhill, What is Manipulation? In Manipulation: Theory and Practice 50, 72 (Christian Coons and Michael Weber, eds., 2014). Barnhill's own account is more subtle.

5. Nudges exploit behavioral biases.

Some people object that nudges "exploit" or "take advantage of" behavioral biases. Indeed, some people *define* nudges as exploitation of behavioral biases.[8] That does sound nefarious. But the objection is mostly wrong, and while people can define terms however they wish, this particular definition is a recipe for confusion.

Many nudges make sense, and help people, whether or not a behavioral bias is at work. A GPS is useful for people who do not suffer from any such bias. Disclosure of information is helpful even in the absence of any bias. A default rule simplifies life and can therefore be a blessing whether or not a behavioral bias is involved. As the GPS example suggests, many nudges have the goal of *increasing navigability*—of making it easier for people to get to their preferred destination. Such nudges stem from an understanding that life can be either simple or hard to navigate, and a goal of helpful nudging is to promote simpler navigation.

At the same time, it is true that some nudges counteract behavioral biases, and that some nudges work because of behavioral biases. For example, many human beings tend to suffer from present bias, which means that they give relatively little weight to the long term; many of us suffer from unrealistic optimism, which means that we tend to think that things will turn out better for us than statistical reality suggests. Some nudges try to counteract present bias and optimistic bias—for example, by emphasizing the long-term risks associated with smoking and drinking, or by suggesting the importance of retirement planning. Similarly, default rules work in part because of inertia, which undoubtedly counts as a behavioral bias. But it is misleading—a form of rhetoric, in the not-good sense—to suggest that nudges "exploit" such biases.

6. *Nudges wrongly assume that people are irrational.* Some critics object that nudges are based on a belief that human beings are "irrational," which is both insulting and false.[9] This objection takes different forms.

8 Ricardo Rebonato, *Taking Liberties* (2012).
9 The most peculiar version of this claim comes from a psychologist: "The interest in nudging as opposed to education should be understood against the specific political background in which it emerged. In the US, the public education system is largely considered a failure, and the government tries hard to find ways to steer large sections of the public who can barely read and write. Yet this situation does not apply everywhere." Gerd Gigerenzer, On the Supposed Evidence for Libertarian Paternalism, *Rev. Phil. and Psychol.* 3, 361 (2016). We offer no comment, except to add that we are unaware of any public officials in the US who have tried hard, or at all, or ever, "to find ways to steer large sections of the public who can barely read and write."

In one form, the objection is that while people rely on simple heuristics and rules of thumb, nothing is wrong with that; those heuristics and those rules work well, and so nudging is not needed, and can only make things worse. In another form, the objection urges that the whole idea of nudging is based on weak psychological research and on an assortment of supposed laboratory findings that do not hold in the real world. In yet another form, the objection is that people can and should be educated rather than nudged.

In its best form, the objection urges that people's utility functions are complex and that outsiders may not understand them; what seems to be "irrationality" may be the effort to trade off an assortment of goals. A mundane example: People might eat fattening foods not because they suffer from present bias, but because they greatly enjoy those foods. A less mundane example: People might fail to save for retirement not because they suffer from optimistic bias, but because they need the money now.

No one should doubt that heuristics generally work well (that is why they exist); but they can also misfire. When they do, a nudge can be exceedingly helpful. Many nudges are developed with reference to well-established behavioral findings, demonstrating that people depart from perfect rationality. For example, default rules work in part because of the power of inertia; reminders are necessary and effective in part because people have limited attention; information will be more likely to influence behavior if it is presented in a way that is attentive to people's imperfect information-processing capacities. These and other claims are based on evidence, both in the laboratory and the real world. (It is always possible that they will be found to be imprecisely stated, or wrong in important settings.) But those who embrace nudges do not use the term "irrationality." In fact they abhor it; "bounded rationality" is much better. Nor does anyone doubt that education can work. As we have emphasized, many nudges are educative. More ambitious educative efforts, such as efforts to help people to assess risks and to teach statistical literacy, are usually complements to nudges, and rarely substitutes or alternatives.

It is also true (and exceedingly important) that people's utility functions are complex and that outsiders might not understand them; that is one reason why nudgers insist on preserving freedom of choice. To the extent that nudging is inevitable, it is pointless to contend that because of the complexity of people's utility functions, nudging should be avoided. To the extent that nudging is optional, it should be undertaken with an appreciation of the risk of error and with careful efforts to ensure that it promotes, and does not undermine, people's welfare. A GPS device does not decrease welfare. In general, information about health risks and potential financial burdens should increase welfare.

Of course nudges must be tested to ensure that they are doing what they are supposed to do. Some nudges fail. When they do, the right conclusion may be that freedom worked—or that we should nudge better.

7. Nudges work only at the margins; they cannot achieve a great deal.

If experts are asked to catalog the world's major problems, many of them would single out poverty, malnutrition and hunger, unemployment, corruption, diseases, terrorism, and climate change. On one view, nudges are an unfortunate distraction from what might actually help. With an understanding of nudging, we might have some fresh ideas about how to tweak letters from government to citizens, producing statistically significant increases in desirable behavior. But that is pretty small stuff. If behavioral economists want to make a contribution, shouldn't they focus on much more important matters?

It is true that behaviorally informed approaches are hardly limited to nudges; mandates, bans, and incentives may well have behavioral justifications. The policy program of behavioral science is not exhausted by nudges.[10] It is also true that some nudges produce only modest changes. But in multiple domains, nudges have proven far more cost-effective than other kinds of interventions, which means that per dollar spent, they have had a significantly larger impact.[11]

By any measure, the consequences of some nudges are not properly described as modest. As a result of automatic enrollment in free school meals programs, more than 11 million poor American children are now receiving free breakfast and lunch during the school year. Credit card legislation, enacted in 2010, is saving American consumers more than ten billion US dollars annually; significant portions of those savings come from nudges and nudge-like interventions.[12]

---

10 Richard Thaler, Much Ado About Nudging, *Behavioral Public Policy Blog* (2017), https:// bppblog.com/2017/06/02/much-ado-about-nudging/.

11 Shlomo Benartzi, et al., Should Governments Invest More in Nudging?, *Psychological Science* 28, 1041 (2017).

12 Sumit Agarwal et al., *Regulating Consumer Financial Products: Evidence from Credit Card.* Work. Pap., NBER (2013).

With respect to savings, automatic enrollment in pension programs has pro-duced massive increases in participation rates.[13]

New nudges, now in the early stages or under discussion, could also have a major impact. If the goal is to reduce greenhouse gas emissions, automatic enrollment in green energy can have large effects in many nations.[14] The Earned Income Tax Credit and its variations rank among the world's most effective anti-poverty program, but many eligible people do not take advantage of it. Automatic enrollment would have large conse-quences for the lives of millions of people. With respect to the most serious problems, the use of nudges remains in its preliminary stages. We will see far more in the future, and the impact will not be small.

It is true, of course, that for countless problems, nudges are hardly enough. They cannot eliminate poverty, unemployment, and corruption. But by itself, any individual initiative—whether it is a tax, a subsidy, a mandate, or a ban—is unlikely to solve large problems. Denting them counts as an achievement.

13 Raj Chetty et al., Active vs. Passive Decisions and Crowdout in Retirement Savings Accounts: Evidence from Denmark, available at www.nber.org/papers/w18565 (2012); Richard Thaler, Much Ado About Nudging., Behavioral Public Policy Blog, https://bppblog.com/2017/06/02/much-ado-about-nudging/ (2017).
14 Felix Ebeling and Sebastian Lotz, Domestic Uptake of Green Energy Promoted by Opt-Out Tariffs, Nature Climate Change 5, 868 (2015), available at doi: 10.1038/nclimate2681; Daniel Pichert and Konstantinos Katsikopoulos, Green Defaults: Information Presentation and Pro-environmental Behaviour, Journal of Environmental Psychology 28, 63 (2008).

9

A BILL OF RIGHTS FOR NUDGING

The idea of "legitimacy," central to contemporary legal theory and political philosophy, can be taken in two different ways. It can be seen as a purely descriptive term: Does the citizenry actually believe that a government or a policy is legitimate? It can also be seen as a normative term: Is a government or a policy legitimate in principle? Under either understanding, of course, the notion of legitimacy needs further specification. But however the notion is specified, it captures the view that governments and policies need to receive, and should deserve to receive, some kind of consent from those who are subject to them. Constitutions are often designed to promote legitimacy in both the descriptive and the normative sense. Bills of Rights, frequently included in constitutions, sometimes define the idea of political legitimacy.

Discussions of legitimacy sometimes focus on the topic of individual rights, emphasizing freedom of speech, freedom of religion, and the right to due process of law. We could easily imagine nudges that would compromise such rights; consider, for example, a default rule that presumed that citizens were Christians, and that they intended to vote for the current leader.

Discussions of legitimacy also focus more broadly on the topic of coercion, and in particular on coercion from government, which has a monopoly on the legitimate use of force. *How can government legitimately require citizens to act or to refrain from acting?* Serious answers draw on a range of philosophical traditions. Whether Kantian, Aristotelian, Lockean, or Benthamite, those answers converge on the view that it is legitimate to prevent harm to others (and thus to forbid murder, assault, or rape) and to solve collective action problems (and thus to provide for national defense and to combat pollution). Many nudges help in those endeavors, but it is generally agreed that they are not sufficient; they are complementary to more aggressive approaches, including uses of the criminal law.

We could easily distinguish among nudges in terms of the kind of problem that they are intended to solve: harm-to-others nudges; collective action problem nudges; coordination problem nudges; harm-to-self nudges. Some of the nudges tested here involve harm to others; consider automatic enrollment in green energy. It is also important to see that behaviorally informed approaches need not be nudges.

For example, a tax on sugary beverages might be defended as a way of counteracting present bias and unrealistic optimism on the part to consumers, and thus of protecting them against their own errors. Fuel economy and energy efficiency standards might be justified as a way of protecting consumers against their tendency to neglect the long term. In a succinct account in 2012, the United States Environmental Protection Agency referred to "inadequate consumer attention to long-term effects of their decisions, or a lack of salience of benefits such as fuel savings to consumers at the time they make purchasing decisions."[1] In a longer account in 2010, the EPA said this[2]:

> The central conundrum has been referred to as the Energy Paradox in this setting (and in several others). In short, the problem is that consumers appear not to purchase products that are in their economic self-interest. There are strong theoretical reasons why this might be so:
>   – Consumers might be myopic and hence undervalue the long-term.
>   – Consumers might lack information or a full appreciation of information even when it is presented.

---

1 See 2017 and Later Model Year Light-Duty Vehicle Greenhouse Gas Emissions and Corporate Average Fuel Economy Standards, Final Rule, 77 Fed. Reg. 62624, 63114, (2012), available at www.gpo.gov/fdsys/pkg/FR-2012-10-15/pdf/2012-21972.pdf.

2 See Light-Duty Vehicle Greenhouse Gas Emission Standards and Corporate Average Fuel Economy Standards; Final Rule, Part II, 75 Fed. Reg. 25,324, 25,510–11 (May 7, 2010), available at www.gpo.gov/fdsys/pkg/FR-2010-05-07/pdf/2010-8159.pdf. Under President Donald Trump, the EPA has proposed to repudiated this analysis and asked for public comments on how to think about consumer savings.

— Consumers might be especially averse to the short-term losses associated with the higher prices of energy efficient products relative to the uncertain future fuel savings, even if the expected present value of those fuel savings exceeds the cost (the behavioral phenomenon of "loss aversion").

— Even if consumers have relevant knowledge, the benefits of energy-efficient vehicles might not be sufficiently salient to them at the time of purchase, and the lack of salience might lead consumers to neglect an attribute that it would be in their economic interest to consider.

We offer these examples only to suggest the wide range of approaches that might emerge from an engagement with behavioral findings. Our own surveys explore only a subset of those approaches. Nonetheless, we think that they tell us a great deal about principles of legitimacy—most obviously in the descriptive sense, but if we have any faith at all in the wisdom of crowds, in the normative sense as well. Many governments are bound by constitutions, of course, and constitutional understandings might well restrict behaviorally informed approaches. For example, the German Constitution requires respect for "human dignity," and in that nation, all such approaches must be consistent with that requirement. The United States Constitution requires states to provide "equal protection of the laws," understood as a broad prohibition on discrimination; nudges, like mandates and bans, could run afoul of that prohibition.

Toward a Bill of Rights for Nudging

Drawing on our findings, we suggest six principles of legitimacy—a kind of Bill of Rights for Nudging. We emphasize that as for other Bills of Rights, the items on the list should be taken as broad principles, rather than as concrete specifications. They remain to be given concrete content through engagement with particular cases. In some cases, they should be treated only as presumptive, and as subject to override on the basis of a compelling justification. For example, the right to freedom of speech does not include bribery, perjury, or criminal conspiracy, and under emergency conditions, the police do not need to get a warrant before searching a home. Nonetheless, the rights to freedom of speech, and to protection from unreasonable searches and seizures, have immense importance. We think that the same is true of the items on this list—understanding them as directed at public officials who nudge, and not for judicial enforcement.

Public officials must promote legitimate ends

People approve of nudges that promote legitimate ends; they disapprove of nudges that promote illegitimate ends. In terms of designing any Bill of Rights, that simple intuition is an excellent place to start.

A mandate, a ban, or a tax might be an effort to insulate public officials and to protect their power; consider a prohibition on dissent. A nudge could easily fall in the same category. We could easily imagine a nudge that would be designed to discourage dissent. As we have seen, the vast majority of Americans reject nudges of this kind, and we expect that the same would be true in most and perhaps all of the nations explored here. Apart from self-insulation, nudges could be designed to protect racial, ethnic, or religious majorities, or to favor men over women. They could be designed to undermine liberty. Such nudges would run afoul of the requirement of legitimate ends.

The issue becomes more interesting, of course, when there is a dispute about what counts as a legitimate end. Is it legitimate to nudge people to be heterosexual? To believe in God? Different people, and majorities in different nations, are likely to offer different answers to such questions, and to many people, the answers are obvious; they essentially need no defense. Our goal here is not, of course, to reach conclusions about what count as legitimate ends. It is only to suggest that insofar as there is legal or social clarity on that topic, it creates a barrier against some nudges.

Nudges must respect individual rights

This idea can easily be seen as a corollary of the prohibition on the pursuit of legitimate ends, but it deserves separate recognition. It is meant to create a kind of second-order right—a right to ensure respect for rights. As we have emphasized, nudges respect freedom of choice, which will often make it harder to see them as rights violations. But our surveys, and some imaginable variations, show that even when nudges allow people to go their own way, they may violate rights. We would not support the design of ballots by which current leaders print their name in big, bold, pleasing letters, and their opponents' names in small, obscure, ugly letters. A political leader may certainly campaign on his own behalf, and use behavioral strategies to nudge people to vote for him; but he may not create a voting system by which those who fail to vote at all are counted as having voted for him.

It remains necessary, of course, to specify the category of individual rights, and to decide whether nudges interfere with them. Different nations may arrive at different judgments on that question. But the general point is clear.

Nudges must be consistent with people's values and interests

Most of the nudges tested here are designed to protect people against their own errors; consider calorie labels, anti-smoking campaigns, and automatic enrollment in savings programs. The overwhelming majority of respondents embrace nudges when they are consistent with people's values and interests—and reject them when they are not.

This principle too can be specified in many different ways, and we could easily imagine cross-cultural variations in the preferred specification. Is it legitimate to attempt to nudge women to embrace traditional gender roles? We do not think so, but there is hardly an international consensus on that score. What matters, for our purposes, is the apparent consensus on the general principle, though different specifications would be intriguing to elicit.

We add as well that the principle is emphatically not designed to forbid public officials from leading rather than following public opinion. In some cases, officials might believe, for example, in protection against discrimination on the basis of ethnicity or religion, and might insist on nudging people not to discriminate on those grounds even if they believe that such discrimination is consistent with their values and very much in their interests. The question whether and when public officials should be able to depart from what (some or many) people believe to be their values or their interests is obviously a delicate one, turning on the grounds on which the departure might be justified. Such officials certainly have a burden of justification. We notice the issue without resolving it here.

Nudges must not manipulate people

In most nations, official manipulation of citizens encounters a kind of taboo, and it often has a constitutional source. In diverse nations, we have found widespread (though not universal) disapproval of subliminal advertising, even when it is meant to achieve legitimate ends. The disapproval might well be rooted in a commitment to individual agency: People are entitled to make up their own minds, exercising their own faculties, and it is not permissible for officials to try to manipulate them. Indeed, it is possible that some people would disapprove of manipulation where they would approve of coercion. We expect that many people who would be willing to accept, or even embrace, a prohibition on the use of drugs (cocaine or heroin) would disapprove of an official effort to use subliminal advertising for that purpose.

We have stressed that the idea of manipulation is not self-defining. There is an elaborate philosophical literature on the subject, with an emphasis on efforts to subvert or undermine, or at least a failure to respect, people's capacity for reflective choice.[3] In addition, some people, committed to some version of utilitarianism, would not impose a taboo on manipulation; they would allow it if it is appropriate or necessary to increase social welfare.[4] Let us bracket the complexities here and note only that in most of the nations explored here, manipulation creates serious concern, and there is at least a presumptive principle against it.

In general, nudges should not take things from people, and give them to others, without their explicit consent

A principle of this general kind does emerge from our findings; consider widespread disapproval of charitable donations by default and of making people organ donors by default. For that reason, it must be included, but it should be treated with considerable caution as we do not know its boundary conditions. For example, most people do not oppose the tax system, even though people do not pay taxes voluntarily. In some nations, military service is obligatory, and that obligation seems to run afoul of the principle. We are not sure whether majority opposition to charitable donations by default is a product of a principle of this kind, or a narrower understanding that charitable donations must be understood as *donations*, that is, an intentional gift from one person to another. If so, the idea of charitable donations by default is objectionable for that very reason.

---

3 For a number of instructive treatments, see *Manipulation* (Christian Coons and Michael Webster, eds., 2014).
4 See Jonathan Baron, A Welfarist Approach to Manipulation, *Journal of Marketing Behavior* 1, 283 (2016).

Nudges should be transparent rather than hidden

The widespread opposition to subliminal advertising is most naturally taken as a prohibition on manipulation, but it can also be taken to support a related principle, which is that nudges, like other interventions, should not be hidden or covert. While our findings do not compel the conclusion that citizens would embrace that principle, we like it, and so we include it here.

Like the previous principles, it requires specification. Transparent about what? A sweet-free cashiers area is obviously transparent in a relevant sense; the area has no sweets. Must it also be transparent in the sense that public officials justify the nudge by reference to the behavioral findings that underpin it? We think that the answer is "yes"—both to ensure that the justification is subject to public scrutiny (and so corrected if it is wrong) and also to treat citizens with respect.

An important qualification involves randomized controlled trials. Many nudges, and many other interventions, are tested in that way, by comparing the outcome of a control condition with that of a treatment condition (in which people might be nudged). While a trial is ongoing, it would likely be self-defeating to disclose its existence to participants. In that sense, transparency is not required. But after the trial has taken place, it is important not to hide it, and to ensure that people generally (and participants in particular) are able to learn what happened. Some kind of public registry might be a good idea for that purpose.

Of welfare and autonomy

A Bill of Rights for Nudging grows fairly directly out of our empirical findings. There are, of course, broader questions about how to evaluate behaviorally informed policies, going well beyond the idea of a Bill of Rights. We close with two candidates. The first involves autonomy. The second involves welfare. The two candidates have powerful theoretical foundations in the Western political tradition; they resonate in other political traditions as well.

The idea of autonomy is of course sharply contested, and we want to avoid controversial philosophical claims here. Does autonomy require freedom of choice? Always? Does it require us to attend to the background conditions under which people form their preferences and values?[5] If so,

---

5 For relevant discussion, see Jon Elster, *Sour Grapes* (1983).

what exactly does that mean? Does it mean that we should dismiss or fail to respect judgments that are based on a lack of information or that come from a problem of self-control?[6] Are some judgments nonautonomous?

Let us bracket these questions. Note first that insofar as we are speaking of nudges, autonomy is preserved in an important sense: People are allowed to do as they wish. They are not forbidden or coerced. But the discussion thus far—and some of our central findings—should be sufficient to show that this is not enough. If people are deceived or manipulated, it is fair to say that their autonomy has been violated. We can also imagine a default rule that would be questionable on grounds of autonomy, and it is now possible to see why. If people lose some right (say, to religious freedom) or some interest (say, to their property) by default, it might well be right to say that their autonomy has been compromised. And if people have not been clearly informed that they have a right to opt out, a default rule might not be altogether different from a mandate or a ban. This point suggests that if autonomy matters, we need to attend closely to the circumstances that allow opt-in or opt-out. Insofar as opt-out rights are concealed, and insofar as opting out is difficult or surrounded by serious burdens, a default rule might undermine autonomy even if it preserves freedom of choice.

The idea of welfare is also contested, and here too, we bracket philosophical disagreements.[7] Does it refer to utilitarianism, narrowly conceived? How shall we define "utility"? Does it refer to pleasures and pains?[8] Does it make distinctions among qualitatively different goods (a beach, a house, a dog, a friendship)? If we can answer such questions, how do we measure welfare? If it is a broader concept than utility (as many think), does it capture everything that ought to matter in human life? If wealthy people lose more than poor people gain, has welfare been reduced? Is that decisive?

Here again we bracket fundamental questions. We suggest that as a general rule, all nudges should have to pass a social welfare test, which means that they should produce welfare gains on net. They should also (and this is an independent point) maximize social welfare, which means that of those approaches that would produce net gains, they should have the highest net gains.

6 A superb collection, with many behavioral insights, is *Addiction and Choice* (Nick Heather and Gabriel Segal, eds., 2017).
7 *See Utilitarianism and Beyond* (Amartya Sen and Bernard Williams et al., 1982).
8 A valuable treatment is Paul Dolan, *Happiness by Design* (2016).

To be more concrete: Suppose that in some nation (say, Norway) a default in favor of green energy would impose significant costs on consumers, because the cost of green energy is higher than that of (say) coal. Suppose too that the green energy default would produce significant reductions in pollution (including greenhouse gas emissions). The questions would be: Are the costs lower than the benefits? If so, are there ways to produce higher net benefits? We could easily imagine cases in which these questions would be easy to answer, because the numbers are so clear. We could also imagine cases in which these questions would be hard. If they turn out to be hard, at least we know why they are hard—and we know where we need to seek more information (or perhaps make some controversial judgments).

We are acutely aware that these points raise immediate questions. Consider five:

1. Nudges should be effective and cost-effective. That seems important. Does our analysis include those requirements?
2. Social welfare is one thing; cost–benefit analysis is another. While cost–benefit analysis is often defended as the most administrable way to test the question whether a policy promotes social welfare, some people are not persuaded at all by that argument.[9] Monetizing various welfare effects can be a serious challenge.
3. Some nudges are designed to overcome present bias and inertia, and the welfare analysis may not be straightforward in such cases. Automatic enrollment in savings programs is an example. If people lose something in take-home pay but have more money in retirement, are they better off?
4. Some nudges are designed to serve distributive purposes. For example, they might be meant to help those at the bottom of the economic ladder. Does the welfare analysis capture that goal?
5. Some nudges are designed to prevent discrimination or to reduce various forms of unfairness. For example, they might be meant to reduce discrimination on the basis of race or sex, or to ensure fair treatment in the workplace. Does the idea of welfare include or exclude that goal?

Some of these questions are easier than others. If a nudge is ineffective, it is unlikely to be delivering significant benefits—which means that it will be exceedingly hard to justify on welfare grounds. The advantage of welfare

9 See Matthew Adler, *Welfare and Fair Distribution* (2011).

analysis is that it forces us to ask the right question: *How effective, exactly?* The idea of cost-effectiveness is important, and the idea of maximizing social welfare captures it in exactly the right way. If an intervention is not cost-effective, it is unlikely to maximize welfare. Some other approach would be better.

Cost–benefit analysis is indeed a proxy for welfare, not the thing itself. In some cases, it might mislead us, or it might prove incomplete—as, for example, when we are dealing with variables that are hard to quantify (such as the effects of disclosure of information).[10] When the goal is to combat present bias or inertia, it remains necessary to ask: Are people being helped or hurt by the nudge, on balance? We cannot evaluate automatic enrollment in pension programs, or think about default contribution rates, without asking that question. We should be aware that despite our best efforts, our answers may be fallible—which presents a reason to engage the public (see Chapter 6).

When the goal is to help those at the bottom of the economic ladder, or to combat discrimination and unfairness, it remains important to know that the intervention is effective and cost-effective. If it would accomplish little or nothing, and if another approach would do as much for a lower cost, then we know enough not to undertake it. But it is not unreasonable to wonder whether the welfare criterion allows us to take account of efforts to help those who face economic deprivation, or sex discrimination, or unfair treatment of workers.

There is a large literature on how to understand welfare and welfarism, with particular attention to exactly these questions. Once more, we do not mean to take a stand on the philosophical questions.[11] We agree that if welfarism is unable to embrace the relevant goals, so much the worse for welfarism; it stands condemned as incomplete.

But our goal here is not to give a full account of the occasions for using nudges or of the proper scope of behaviorally informed tools. We emphasize more modestly the importance of respecting autonomy and of promoting social welfare. These ideas fit, broadly speaking, with our empirical findings. We have not said that the results of surveys should be taken as decisive. On the contrary, we have emphasized that judgments about potential policies demand a careful study of their likely effects—and that public judgments, uninformed as they may be, are no substitute for that kind of study.

10 For detailed discussion, see Cass R. Sunstein, *The Cost–Benefit Revolution* (2018).
11 See Adler, *supra* note 130.

Nonetheless, we confess that we have been singularly impressed with what we have found—and in important respects, surprised by our findings. The judgments of ordinary citizens suggest an intuitive understanding, in diverse nations, of the importance of both autonomy and welfare. They suggest that in this domain, as in many others, any Bill of Rights will not be a top-down imposition from a self-appointed political elite. It is more likely to be an outgrowth of powerful strands in national cultures, and perhaps even the human heart.

ACKNOWLEDGMENTS

This book has been years in the making, and we have many institutions and individuals to thank.

For financial support, we are grateful to the Behavioral Economics and Public Policy Program at Harvard Law School; we are also grateful to the Governing Responsible Business Cluster at Copenhagen Business School and the Center for Consumption, Markets and Politics at Zeppelin University in Germany. For valuable discussions at various stages, we thank Eric Posner, Eldar Shafir, and Richard Thaler. For invaluable research support we thank Micha Kaiser and Julius Rauber. For editorial assistance and research support, we thank Andrew Heinrich. Special thanks go to Roger Franz for his valuable suggestions.

We also thank the cooperators and governments of Flanders (Belgium), Ireland, and Mexico for sharing their national survey data with us.

In producing this book, we have drawn on a series of studies on public opinion and behaviorally informed approaches. Though we have made significant changes and additions, we are grateful for permission from the following journals. For Chapters 1, 2, and 3, "Do People Like Nudges?," *Administrative Law Review*; for Chapter 4, "Do Europeans Like Nudges?," *Judgment and Decision Making* 11, 310 (2016); for Chapter 5, "A Global Consensus on Nudging? Almost But Not Quite," *Regulation and Governance* 12, 3 (2018); for Chapter 6, "Trusting Nudges? Lessons From An International Survey," *Journal of European Public Policy*

(DOI: 10.1080/13501763.2018.1531912; for Chapter 8, "Misconceptions About Nudges," *Journal of Behavioral Economics for Policy* 2, 61 (2018).

Early discussions of some of our findings are also reported in Cass R. Sunstein, *The Ethics of Influence* (2016) and Cass R. Sunstein, *Human Agency and Behavioral Economics* (2017); in all cases, we draw on the original sources, not on the material that appears there.

INDEX

Entries in **bold** denote tables; entries in *italics* denote figures.

abortion: attitudes to nudges on 9, 23; educative and noneducative nudges on 98–100, 108–12, **110,** 118

active choice, mandatory 40

affirmative consent *see* explicit consent

age, and attitude to nudging 65

agency: and educative nudges 95, 97, 99–100, 103–4, 108, 116–18; nudges as insult to 119–20

alcohol consumption 71–2, 74, 77, 83

American exceptionalism 29

attention filtering 57

Australia, attitudes to nudging in 63

autonomy, and nudging 4–5, 7, 116, 134–5, 137–8

behavioral biases 96, 120–1, 124

Behavioural Insights Team (UK) 1–2

Belgium 71, 73–4, 82, 84

benefit-cost analysis 43, 115, 117, 136–7

Bill of Rights for Nudging x, 30, 130–4

BMI (Body Mass Index) 71–2, 76

boosts 97

bounded rationality 125

Brazil: attitudes to nudging in 63; use of nudging in 66n9

BRICS countries 53–4

Buchanan, James 120–1

cafeteria design 22, 99, 108–10, 122

calorie labels 2n6: European attitudes to 35, **38,** 39; partisan differences on 24; targeting of 83; US attitudes to 9, **10**

Cameron, David 28

Canada, attitudes to nudging in 62, 66

carbon emissions charge 15–16, 35, **39**, 40, 66

cautiously pro-nudge nations 55, 66, 70, 73, 82

charitable donations, default rules for 11, 16, 22, 30, 35, **39**, 40, 44, 60, 66, 133

children: educative and noneducative nudges for 99–100, 108–12; number of 57, 79

China, attitudes to nudging in 54–5, 60–3, 67–9, 80

choice architecture 2, 4; European attitudes to 35, 43; global attitudes to 62; mandatory active choice as 40; motivations behind 19, 28; US attitudes to 12–13

choice editing 35

cigarette package warnings 9, 24

Citizens Score 68

clean energy see green energy

coercion 128–9, 133

Communism, warning labels for 17–18, 22

consumption habits 72, 74, 83

correlation heatmap 75, 76

credit card legislation 126

cultural clusters 54, 71

default rules 2, 7; and agency 120; European attitudes to 30, 35, **39**, 40–1, 43; global attitudes to 60, 61; law as 121; as noneducative nudge 95, 97; people disadvantaged by 21; transparency about 123; US attitudes to 8, **15**, 16

Denmark, attitude to nudges in 31, 36, 39–40, 42–3, 45–7, 55, 66–7, 82, 86

descriptive statistics **88–9**

dignity 4–5, 116–17, 130

disclosures 22

discrimination, combating 14, 20, 130, 132, 136–7

distracted driving: global attitudes to 59; graphic warnings about 114; public education against 10, 23–4, 35, **37**

distributive purposes 136

Earned Income Tax Credit 127

economic incentives 115

educative nudges 31; and agency 117–19; preference for 98–103, **102**, **105**, **106–7**, **111**, 112–4, **113**; regulators' use of 114–16; and thinking systems 96–7; use of term 95

effectiveness information 98–9, 102, **103–7**, 112, **113**, 115

environmental concern, and nudge approval 72, 75, 83

EPA (Environmental Protection Agency) 129–30

ethical issues 4–6

Europe: attitudes to nudges in **34**, 35–44, **37–41**; items in nudge survey **32–3**; national variations in 29–31, 45–6; political parties of **49–50**

explicit consent, to takings 22, 28, 30, 44, 47, 60, 133

food labeling see calorie labels; traffic light food labeling

formal education, and nudge approval 58, 79

framing, of ethical questions 5
France, attitude to nudges in
    31, 46–7
free school meals programs 126
freedom of choice 119–21, 125, 131,
    134; perceived 74, 76
fuel economy and energy efficiency
    standards 129–30

gender: and attitude to nudges 42,
    47, 63, 75–6, 80, 83, 84–5; changing
    18, 21
Germany, attitude to nudges in 31,
    82, *86*
GFK (Gesellschaft für
    Konsumforschung) 33
GMOs (genetically modified
    organisms) 9n2, 12–13, 22
green energy: educative and
    noneducative nudges 98, 100–8,
    112; encouraged or mandated
    use of **12**, 20, 35, **39**, 40–1, 60, 79,
    114, 127
green nudges 72
Green Parties 46–7

Hayek, Friedrich 120–1
health warnings, graphic 9n4, 97,
    101–3, 114–15, 123
healthy food placement **12**, **39**, 40,
    58, 61
heuristics 27, 67, 96, 125
Hungary, attitudes to nudges in
    31, 36, 39, 42–3, 45, 47, 55,
    66–7, 70

illicit goals 4, 7, 19–20, 53
India 54n1
individual rights 6, 128, 131–2

inertia: and default rules 97, 117,
    124–5; negative consequences of 7,
    22, 28, 44
information nudges 35, **37–8**, 39–40,
    42, 46, 65
Internet penetration rates 54
intrusiveness, levels of *see* nudge
    clusters
Ireland 82, 84
irrationality, nudges as assuming
    124–6
Italy, attitude to nudges in 31, 36, 40,
    42, 45

Japan, attitudes to nudges in 55, 60,
    62–3, 66–7, 69–70

Kahneman, Daniel 95–6
knowledge problem 120–1

labor violations, labels for 14, 22
legitimacy: of goals 9, 23, 30, 43, 47,
    131; of nudging 7, 82–3, 128–30
loss aversion 30, 60, 130

mandates: and nudges 114, 117; US
    attitudes to 24–5
manipulation: nudges as acceptable
    123; protection against 121;
    unacceptable 22–3, 30, 44, 53, 114,
    132–3
markets, belief in 76–7, 83
meat-free days 35, **41**, 42, 63, 65, 77, 83
Mexico 82, 84

name changes, automatic 13–16,
    20, 53
noneducative nudges 31; and agency
    117–18; and freedom of choice 120;

preference for 98–100, **102–6**,
111, 112–4, **113**; regulators' use of
114–16; and thinking systems 97;
use of term 95
nudge clusters: in European survey
35–6, 43; in global survey 59, 64,
78–9, 82–4, **93–4**
nudges: costs of 116; covertness
of 122–3; effectiveness of 126–7;
institutional use of 2–4; national
categories of support for 55, 65–9;
objectives of 129; public opinion
on 4–7; use of term 1–2

Obama, Barack 3, 26
obesity, educative and noneducative
nudges on 98–9, 109, **110–11**
obesity education: European
attitudes to 35, **37**; global attitudes
to 59; partisan differences on 24;
US attitudes to 10–11, 20, 23–4
opioid addiction 121, 123
optimism, unrealistic 124, 129
order effects 14, 95, 112
organ donors: default rule for 13n13;
mandatory active choice **12**, 21, 35,
39, 40, 61–2, 66n9
overeating, public education about
11, 35, **37**
overwhelmingly pro-nudge nations
55, 67, 69, 73, 82

Park Geun-hye 69
partisan nudge bias 25–8, 73
paternalism 30, 46
political attitudes: educative and
noneducative nudges and 106–8,
110–2, **111**, 117; in European survey

33, 36, 46, **51**; in global survey 57–8,
64, 65, 73; in US survey 9, 11–12,
20, 22–4
political parties, nudges favoring 15,
18–19
political valence, of nudges 7, 26–7
preference falsification 68–9
present bias 96, 124–5, 129, 136–7
principled pro-nudge nations 55,
65–6, 70, 73, 82
public choice problems 120–1
public education campaigns:
European attitudes to 36, **37–8**;
global survey on 59–60; US
attitudes to 8, 10, **11**, **17**, 18, 20–1

Qualtrics 56
quantitative information 103–6, **104**,
107, 110, 117

randomized controlled trials 122, 134
reactance 98n8, 123
Red Cross *see* charitable donations,
default rules for
relevant information 6, 43, 97, 115
religion, nudges favoring 15–16, 19
risk aversion 72–3, 76
Russia: attitudes to nudging in 54–5,
62–3, 66; use of nudging in 66n9

salt content labels **12**, 13, 22, 35, **38**, 39
sampling: for European survey 31, **48**;
for global surveys 56–7, **70**, 73–4,
87, **90–2**
savings plans: automatic enrolment
in 9–10, 20, 24–5, 101, 114,
122, 127, 136; educative and
noneducative nudges 98, 100–8

self-government 4, 6–7
sexual orientation discrimination
 10–11
'significantly more effective' *see*
 effectiveness information
smoking: educative and
 noneducative nudges 98, 100–8;
 and nudge approval 71, 74, 77, 83;
 public education about 11, 35, **37**
social welfare 5–6, 84, 115, 133, 135–7
sociodemographic variables: in
 Europe 35–6, 42–3, 47, **51–2**; in
 global survey 57–8, 63, **64**
South Africa, attitudes to nudging
 in 63
South Korea, attitude to nudges in
 55, 60–2, 67–70, 82–3, 86
statistical literacy 97, 125
subliminal advertising: European
 attitudes to 30, 35, **40**, 42, 44, 47;
 global attitudes to 62, 63, 114, 123,
 132, 134; US attitudes to 9, 17, 114
sugar taxes 129
sweet-free cashier zones 31, 35, **41**,
 42, 45, 63, 65, 134
System 1 nudges *see* noneducative
 nudges
System 2 nudges *see* educative
 nudges
Systems 1 and 2 thinking *see* thinking
 systems

takings 21
Tannenbaum, David 25–7, 45n8
terrorism, warning labels for 14, 22
test-learn-adapt-share approach 84
thinking systems 95–7; and nudge
 preference 114

traffic light food labeling **12**, 24, 32,
 38, 39, 66n9
transparency 122–3, 134
trust: in government 47, 67, 70, 73–5,
 120–2; institutional 71–2, 74–6, 77,
 79, 80–1, 83; in other people 76;
 social 71–2, 74, 76

United Kingdom: attitudes to nudges
 in 31, 36, 40, 42, 45; partisan
 differences on nudging 46; use of
 nudges in 2, 28, 30
United States: attitudes to nudging
 in 8–19, **10–13**, **17**, 82; preference
 for educative and noneducative
 nudges in 98–112; use of nudging
 in 2–3
utilitarianism 133, 135
utility functions, complexity of 125

values and interests, consistency
 with 8, 22, 114, 132
visual illusions 9, 22, 114
voter registration: automatic
 13–14, 20; educative and
 noneducative nudges 98–9,
 108–12, **109**, **111**

warnings 2; US attitudes to 8
water conservation, educative and
 noneducative nudges 98, 100–8,
 117–18
welfare analysis, of nudging 115–16,
 135–8
women's surnames *see* name
 changes, automatic
World Bank, use of nudging 3
WVS (World Values Survey) 72, 74

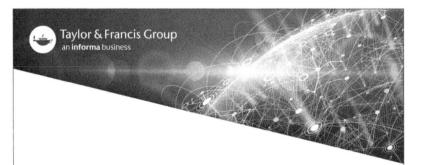